THE
WALK
I TOOK

My Biography

Lori P. Cameron

WB WRITERS'
BRANDING

Writers' Branding
1-877-608-6550
www.writersbranding.com
media@writersbranding.com

CONTENTS

DEDICATION

This book is dedicated to my Lord and Saviour, Jesus Christ.

My precious Lamb of God, who has covered me with His blood and led me on a wonderful journey. The still small voice of the Holy Spirit, who has guided me through so many precarious times in my life.

For God, my Abba Father, who gave His only begotten Son to redeem me and a multitude of other men and women in the world who believe in Him.

I will praise Him amid the congregation, testify of His unconditional love that He has shown towards me, tell of the faith of Jesus for all to hear, and come to know as their own personal Saviour. Praise the Lord, Amen.

FOREWORD

This book is for all those dear men, women, and children who have suffered at the hands of men and women who want coercive control over them. I pray this book is a blessing to you all whatsoever you have suffered through and be inspired to know there is a light at the end of the tunnel.

This is a genuinely inspirational testimony of what Jesus has done in the life of Lori Cameron.

PROLOGUE

If I had only known that the Lord was my Shepherd and that Jesus loves His little children, how different might my life have been?

Knowing that we are children of God, and He wants to lead and guide us in our lives.

I wonder how children's lives might have been different knowing that somebody loved them, children who longed for a hug, a tender word, had the comfort of knowing a loving parent.

Jesus says, "Come unto me, all ye that labour and are heavily laden, and I will give you rest. Take my yoke upon you, and learn of me, for I am meek and lowly in heart: and you shall find rest unto your souls. For my yoke is easy, and my burden is light." Matthew 11.28-30 KJV

Come unto Jesus, for the road I travelled, in the end, was never lonely, my Saviour has always been with me, for I held on to Him and never let go.

CHAPTER 1

THE GROWING YEARS

I grew up near the beautiful coast of Dublin in Ireland. There was beauty outside; however, there was darkness in the home. My earliest memories were not at all pleasant. My mother stood at the top of thirteen stairs with me, screaming at my father, "I do not want her; you have her, catch!!" My father was pleading with my mother, "Anna, put her down." Then my voice, screaming, as she threw me down the flight of stairs to my father. My father held me in his arms, trembling at what had happened.

My mother's father was callous to her, and she suffered at his hands. My mother was a hysterical alcoholic and would continue to be like that throughout the years knowing her. Nevertheless, my uncle confided in me how her father had treated her, and I can now look back with understanding, knowing what had caused this.

One summer, sitting on our front steps, my mother said to me, "You were supposed to have been a boy; I would call him Patrick; I never wanted you." My name was Patricia.

My mothers' parents lived at the top of our street. When we visited them this one day, my grandmother said, go and sit on your grandad's knee. Oh, the horrors of what he was doing to me. Unbeknown to my mother or grandmother. I started to squirm, but mum told me to behave myself. My grandfather had his hand in my

1

knickers and was fingering me. This sickening feeling is still with me to this day. I managed to get off his knees and ran to a chair. My mother and grandmother scolded me and told me to get back, but I refused. Pat, you naughty girl, you deserved a good thrashing. Back at home in the kitchen, I tried to tell my mother what grandad had done to me, tears filling my eyes, but my mother rebuked me and told me again that I deserved a good thrashing.

My brother was born when I was four years old, my mother finally got her Patrick, but that was his middle name. I loved my brother right from the beginning; yes, we had our spats; however, that was normal for children.

When I was five years old, I kept getting sick from earaches and a sore throat. Unbeknown to me, arrangements were taking place about this. One day, mum said that grandmother was going to take me on a bus to meet dad and that he was going to take me shopping. I used to love meeting dad and going out with him; however, when we finally got off the bus, dad was not there. "Where is daddy? I asked?" Grandmother pointed to a large building and said he would meet us there. When we reached the building, grandmother rang the bell, and a nurse came out, took me by the hand, and closed the door. I was on my own with this stranger. "Where is my daddy?" I cried; as the nurse led me to a bed, I started screaming. I was so traumatized that I lost my voice. All these strangers around me, I remember other children in their beds lined up to go into this expansive room, filled with lights and strange-looking things; I had my tonsils and adenoids out.

Mum and dad came in the next day with ice cream for me, but I could not talk; it would be long after I was home before speaking again. The trauma had so paralyzed me. Friends would come to play snakes and ladders with me, but I could not talk to them. Then one day, I got out of bed, and a shrill scream came out of my mouth, and I could not stop crying. Then, slowly I started to speak.

My mother enrolled me in the Brownies, which I immensely enjoyed; sometimes, we would get together with the Cub Scouts, it was there that I would meet David. Mum had invited his mum back to our home not to go back to her home, and David and I would walk home from the club house where the Brownies and Cubs would come for the meetings. In one way, you could say that we gradually grew up together. Mum would not let me go into the Girl Guides. During a class at the secondary high school, I was handed a note from one of the girls, and they started to giggle; as I read the message, I saw that it was from David, he wanted to meet with me at the library, and he would be there with his friends.

My mother and father's marriage were not a happy one. There would always be rows and tension at the meal table. My dad kept a carving knife by him at the table, and if my brother or I went to reach across the table to get something, we would have the carving knife slapped across our knuckles.

One day lying in bed, in the room above the living room, my mother was screaming at my father, then suddenly, I heard my father say, "Anna put down the poker." Then I started screaming, thinking my mother would kill my dad. Dad came running into my bedroom; I was crying uncontrollably; dad took me in his arms and said it was all right. I kept saying, mum is going to kill you. "No, Pat, everything is going to be all right. I am here; stop crying," he said as he held me tightly.

After this, I started having nightmares where my mother poisoned my dad. It would always be my dad that would console me. I do not, however, remember my dad ever saying he loved me; nevertheless, he showed me in other ways his love for me. However, I did love my dad. Unfortunately, I could only get so close to him; it was like he had put a wall up around himself. Although dad never talked about the war and what he went through in Africa and the countries he passed through, I am sure he suffered from shell shock or PTSD, the new name for shell shock.

I do not know what mum felt about me. Mum was a tailor, as was her mother a tailor. Mum always made my clothes, and they were beautiful; I cannot fault her for that, even knitting jumpers and cardigans for me. It was very bewildering growing up in that house.

It is extraordinary; I do not remember seeing my brother; it seemed just mum and me at home. If mum did not want to see me, she would lock me up in the dark cupboard under the stairs at the back of the kitchen. Mum would do this so many times. I was terrified; I had always been scared of the dark.

Due to the treatment from my mother, I developed stuttering and nervous shaking of the body. My parents arranged an appointment for me with a child counsellor, who eventually helped.

An older man came live with us from next door when his wife died. As I always called him, Grandad Fox was a kind man, and I enjoyed being with him; we would play dominoes and cribbage and take me out with him sometimes. This one day, Grandad Fox took my brother and me out to the Sports Centre in Dublin. The centre was a vast place and quite lovely to walk around. Walking on top of a steep hill, my brother pushed me, and I fell down the slope, severely injuring my ankle. A lady saw what happened and came up to me as she could see that I was in pain. As Grandad did not have a car, she offered to take us all home. By the time we got home, my ankle was quite swollen, so my dad kept soaking it in icy water to try and bring the swelling down. It was going to take at least six weeks before the ankle healed. My mother insisted that I kept walking on it and did not have any sympathy for me.

My one joy was when I travelled by train to my gran and grandpop down on the farm as a young girl. They were my dad's parents. How I loved them, it was wonderful to go about in the fields; I always felt free as a bird when down on the farm, being with the horses and the cows, helping to muck out; I was in my element. My dad's father, grandpop, was a wonderful old man who always loved being outside; his gardens were amazing. Nan was so lovely and oh, her cooking and baking, the wonderful aromas that crept from the cottage. I always felt safe with them. Their cottage was like a fairy cottage, with lattice windows all around. Inside, you would go through a narrow door to a narrow staircase leading up to the bedrooms; it was like living in a doll's house.

Of a night-time, Grandpop would take his dog out for a walk, and I would go with him; this was such a special time, being with Grandpop, and when we returned, Nan would always have the table laid for sandwiches with fresh lettuce, spring onions, radishes, and drinks for us all.

At ten years of age, I experienced my first period; I was terrified of seeing the blood. I had no idea what was happening to me. I called my mother, who, instead of being understanding, told me if I ever allowed a boy to touch me on my legs, she would kill me and throw me into the river at the end of our road. Mum did not explain to me the changes that were taking place in my body. Mum gave me rags, which she had torn up for me to wear; I would not get sanitary pads until my high school assistant principal became involved.

During this time at secondary high, I had a friend who offered to carry my books home. I never had a boy offering to walk me home before; I was fourteen. Well, my mother was waiting at the garden gate for me, and she was furious when she saw me walking with a boy; mum called me a prostitute, all names she could think of, and I had better not ever let her see me with a boy again. It took her brother, my uncle, to intervene on my behalf and tell her to ease up on me. Shortly after this, my mother enrolled me in classes for ice skating. Eventually, I learned enough to skate correctly; however, my mother did not want me to take dance lessons at the ice rink.

Nevertheless, I continued to go skating, and my father would meet me at the bus stop to bring me home. During this time, I met an ice hockey player who wanted to date me, he was fun to be around, and we dated for about six months; however, he soon tired of me as I refused to have sex with him. If you loved me, you would want to be with me, which boys tend to say to young girls. Anyway, we broke up; yes, I was as distraught as any teenage girl. One day, I was at the ice rink and skating to the music, when these boys came along, the end boy with his hand stretched out for mine was David and his friends. I was so pleased to see him, and from then on, our friendship continued.

I loved to study and do homework and did well in high school and was able to go on to Wesley College for girls in Dublin, which taught the skills needed for office work, such as typing, shorthand, bookkeeping, commerce, and how to dress for business, what colors to wear and what not to wear. There were also elocution classes, which were quite fun, getting your tongue around the sentences, to enable us to speak correctly. I enjoyed college and made friends, and the girls were fun to be around. I passed all my exams, and then, it was off to find a job.

My first job was miserable; I had a Personnel Officer who would continually watch me over my shoulder, which made me nervous and caused me to make mistakes. After three months, I was handed my notice. Distraught at telling my parents that I had lost my job, I went up to David's house as I was afraid to go home. His mum, Janet, is such a warm, loving mother, whom I also loved, gave me a cup of tea, and tried to calm me down. When David and his father came in, His father said, "We must let your parents know where you are." I was scared by this fact; now what would happen, I thought fearfully. My mother had already been angry that I had not gone home to tell her and dad. Did they know how scared I was to say to them that I had lost my job? Both mum and dad were in a storm of anger when they arrived at David's home because I had lost my job. I was never to hear the end of it. Each day, I was handed the newspaper to scan for a job but could not see anything suitable. Finally, my dad spoke to a friend of his who ran a large car parts warehouse and offices, and he offered me a job in the office there. I really enjoyed the work, and the girls were great to work with, so I settled happily into this new job.

By now, I was seventeen, and one day up at my friend David's home, we had seen each other for quite a while, though not genuinely dating, we enjoyed each other's company, going for long bike rides, and going up to his parent's home for tea on Sunday's. One day walking me home, David asked me if I would go to bed with him? I thought to myself, what a funny thing to ask (I was very naïve). I said all right, thinking we would just lay down for a chat or a snooze. We had never even kissed. When the day came, and we went upstairs to his room, he started undressing; I just took off my dress, kept the rest of my clothing on, and got into bed. David was already in bed and said, "Aren't you going to take the rest of your clothes off?" I said, "What for?" Then it hit me; I shot out of that bed like a rocket, put my dress on, and went home. I decided I was not going to see him anymore. However, that did not happen. David was my first love; even though it had been puppy love, I cared about David. When Sunday came around again, I went up as usual for tea. I had bought David a man's grooming set in my naivety, hoping to appease him. He was very sulky when I saw him but decided to ignore this fact. I was not going to sleep with anyone before I married them, and that was that.

We continued, as usual, then one day, I ran into David all dressed up. I said, "Where are you going; all dressed up?" David said that his mum had bought the outfit for him as they were sending him and his friend Stuart off to Butlins Holiday Camp and that he would see me when they got back the following week. The next week after David was home from camp, I went there for tea. David and his dad were grinning at each other. I asked what was going on? I wish I had not requested. David showed me pictures his friend had taken of him with a girl on his lap cuddling him. I could not believe it; I was devastated; they thought it was a big joke. However, I did not and ran out of there all the way home. Hurt and feeling rejected, losing my best friend, was all of which I could think.

The following week, Dad knew how upset I was and asked me, "Would you like to come to the club with me?" I did not want to go anywhere. "Come on," said dad, it will do you good. Get yourself ready, and I will take you. Arriving at the club, as we walked in through the hall, I saw a family there that we knew, who were good friends of our family. I felt easier knowing that there was someone that I knew. Dad and I sat with them and chatted as they introduced a mother and her adult son, Brian, and my friend Jane with her boyfriend, Jim. The music started, and as they got up to dance, Brian asked me to dance with him. At the end of the evening, we arranged to go out as a foursome the next day. (Did I realize that I was jumping out of the frying pan into the fire.

I wish I had not gone out with them; I wish I had given David a second chance, but I had refused to do so. How could I trust him again? In the months and years to follow, I would deeply regret my decision not to trust David. If I had stayed with David, I would not have experienced the hell that was to be my life with Brian.

CHAPTER 2

PORNOGRAPHY

We had dated for a year; when Brian proposed to me, he had already received my parent's blessings. Brian was four years older than me, and at first, I was smitten with him, being on the rebound from David. Little did I know at the time that this relationship would eventually destroy me.

We drove out into the country one day and stopped the car on an old track. I thought to myself, why have we stopped here? There is nothing around? When Brian said to me, "I want to show you something you have not seen before." Next, he undid his pants' zip, pulled out his penis, and asked me to touch it. I was disgusted; I had never seen anything so ugly. I shrank away from him. Thankfully, he did not persist, covered himself up again, and we drove back to my home.

As you are aware, by now, I knew nothing about sex. I did make Brian aware that there would be no intercourse between us before we were married.

The date of our wedding was to be in six months in May so that it would be a spring wedding. My mother warned me to wait three years before having a baby. I took a day off from work to go and buy my trousseau and going away outfit, which I had seen in a store window, it was what I wanted. It was a baby blue wool suit with a fur collar. I had bought the outfit and was walking through the town to buy a matching navy purse, shoes, and gloves to match. Suddenly, I heard a woman shouting and screaming; my mother was yelling from the bus window, shouting at me to go to work and what was I doing in town? I decided to put mum out of my head so that I could enjoy my day. I found the accessories to go with my new suit, then excitedly went into my favourite store to buy my new lingerie. As I went down the street, I saw this beautiful turquoise negligee in the shop window, went inside the shop, and saw how lovely it was, this too I bought. So pleased was I with my purchases, then catching the bus back home. However, I decided to go to Aunty Jeans, who lived two houses from where I lived with mum and dad. She was so pleased to see me, especially when I told her what I had bought. "Let us go up to Joanie's bedroom and lay it all out on the bed," she said. Auntie Jean was as excited as I was when we took everything out and laid it on the bed. I went back home to help dad get dinner ready, and while we were preparing the meal, I told him what I had done that day. Working on the dinner at the stove, mum suddenly burst into the house, yelling and screaming at me for not having gone to work that day, it was so bad that I ran out of the house and ran to Auntie Jean's home, mum came running down the path shouting at me, don't you dare go to that woman's home. I banged on Auntie Jean's door, and when Uncle Bill opened the door and saw the state that I was in, said Jean, get her a brandy quick, Pat is in shock.

My wedding day had arrived, and I put on the gown that Auntie Jean had made for me; it was beautiful, so was the bridesmaid's dress that she had made for Sue, my girlfriend. Dad was beaming as I walked down the stairs of our house. Mum had on a cream-colored suit the same as I had bought. After the wedding, due to heavy fog at the airport, we could not fly out that night, so my uncle arranged for us to stay in a hotel in town. Our wedding night was strange. There was no cuddling or kissing, I did not know what to do, so Brian just got on top of me. I thought, is this making love? I honestly did not know if we had or not. We were to fly to Spain the next day, to friends of Brian's family who had a boarding house there. Instead of coming to bed with me that night, Brian stayed up to play cards with the husband. It was awful. I was upset; the lady came in with a cup of tea for me and looked at me with sympathy. The next day, we met a couple staying at the boarding house; Brian was more interested in them, especially the wife, than he was in me. It was not a good honeymoon.

All married couples on the farm had a house waiting for them. It was beautiful, and the back of the house looked out on hills and valleys. I loved to cook and bake and soon got into the way of a homemaker. One day, Brian asked me to go to the newsagents and pick up a package for him. The news agent was displeased that Brian had sent me to get it for him. Upon arriving home with the package, Brian opened it and showed me what was in the package. It was a book and said to me, I want you to read this book, and I will ask you questions on it tonight.

The book was all pornography, disgusting, is putting it mildly. I was so disgusted as I looked through the pages; the book was sickening. That night he questioned me about what I had read. I felt sick; I did not want to speak in regard to the book, nevertheless, since our wedding, I had learned that I had to do what he said and not argue with him, but in this instance, I was not going to go along with a discussion on pornography. If Brian loved me, he had a strange way of showing it. We had been married for about three months, I was not feeling very well, so I went to the doctor, yes, I was pregnant. I was over the moon, so happy that I was expecting a baby. When I arrived home, Brian was home for his break, so I told him that I was pregnant; he was thrilled that we would be having a baby in the new year. My parents came up for a visit that weekend; I took my dad to the garden and told him that his grandchild was on the way. Dad was delighted; however, mum had watched us from the kitchen window, and when we went into the house, she flew at me and said, "Are you pregnant?" I said yes; she screamed and yelled at me for not doing as she had said and waited the three years. I was devastated and could not stop crying. Poor dad got her out of the house, and they left what my poor dad had to put up with mum. How he managed, I will never know. It turned out that when the doctor said I was pregnant, I wasn't; it was the pill that had messed me up; however, stopping the pill when told that I was pregnant, I conceived, now the baby was not going to be born until much later, according to a Consultant that the doctor sent me to see. When I went into labour, the ambulance took me to a nursing home. However, there were complications. My baby was lying in the wrong position; the doctor tried to manoeuvre the baby around to where it should be but could not do so. They rushed me to the General Hospital.

Nevertheless, it was long labour; my baby boy was born in March. Unfortunately, I had complications afterward. I haemorrhaged severely, and then I had mastitis so that I could not feed my baby; he had to be bottle-fed. My family and friends came to visit me; however, they could only see me outside the hospital window. After two weeks, I was allowed to go home with my baby.

Coming back from a visit with relatives, I was looking at John, and said to Brian, I want another baby, so that they can grow up together. Again, I conceived straight away, and another baby was due again the following year, only April this time. Again, mum and dad came for a visit, up the garden with dad to tell him, of course, he was pleased, however, another story again with mum, she went into a screaming tantrum, it was horrendous. I went to the pantry and broke down; could I never please her. Mum and I never spoke for five months. Dad would come up to visit me on his bike. Poor dad, what he suffered from mum, was nobody's business. I loved my dad so much.

My new baby boy was born in April at home; it was an easy birth this time, and how different were the boys. Ken was a quiet, peaceful baby; I called him my little man and loved him. Life went on, John and Ken were growing, how I love them. We now had a Golden Retriever that needed a new home as her family was going away. The tremendous fun that I would have with our dog and my two boys. I would take the boys and the dog down into the fields by the stream, and we would have a lovely time together. Going over to this area would be our regular daily outing in the summer. The boys were clambering around the trees and sandy playing by the stream; it was relaxing.

Looking back, I do not remember Brian ever playing with John and Ken, and their toys had to be out of sight for when he came in from work. So, he could relax in his chair. Then I became pregnant again, only this time Brian would not acknowledge my pregnancy; this disturbed me. We were in town, and I started having cramps and not feeling well. We went into a store, and I knew I needed to go home; however, Brian would not allow me to. As I rushed for the bathroom the next day, I started losing large blood clumps. I arranged for a neighbor to watch the boys, telling her what was wrong. I went down to the surgery; at the doctors, when he examined me, he said that I was miscarrying and that I was to go to bed when I arrived back home. The baby would take about a week to come out of me. I was so upset that I had lost a baby, mainly because I felt sure that I was expecting a baby girl; I had been knitting for her. When I arrived back home, my news did not go down well, and Brian was not upset for me; he never comforted me, there was no consoling whatsoever. I was affected by this, and I went into a deep depression. Brian decided to have a vasectomy; therefore, no more children.

Where Brian worked, the manager had died, and understandably, Brian thought that the manager's position would go to him; unfortunately, the farmer hired someone from another farm. When Brian heard this news, he was angry, so he started looking for jobs on other farms but to no avail. Finally, his cousin Ken from Canada suggested that we emigrate there, and Ken told Brian what we would need to do. To cut a long story short, the Government accepted us, and a job offer from a farm in Manitoba, Canada, came along for Brian which sounded on paper exceptionally good. In May, we were to sail out from Liverpool on the Princess of Canada. The government arranged for packing for us and all the belongings we would take to go in containers on the ship. The ship was quite lovely, and except for a couple of days of seasickness, we were okay and enjoyed the trip that would take seven days. When we arrived in Manitoba, the farm was not what we had expected, this was not a modern farm, and the house that went with the job had plaster that had come off of the ceiling onto the floor, it was unbelievable and so filthy, and in need of work, it was a total nightmare. We were supposed to have stayed there a year, but we left after a month. Brian's cousin Ken and his wife offered to put us up in their home in Winnipeg until Brian had a permanent job. The job came quickly, and we could move into a rented apartment. Here we stayed a year until we had a down payment on a house in Winnipeg. Brian had a remarkably decent job, and the pay was excellent; however, I wanted to be able to work and have an income of my own. I did not want to go out to work until the boys were at least eleven years old; therefore, I took in sewing and made curtains for a store in town. Then when that ended, I took in typing, which helped me have money of my own.

CHAPTER 3

A DEPRAVED LIFE

Our sex life, I cannot call it making love because it was not, was taking on a more perverse turn. I did not like it. Brian started using play tools on me. I was changing and not for the better, and I was becoming increasingly depressed as if I were not myself anymore. If someone asked me a question, Brian would not let me answer; he would always answer for me. Our neighbors, Derrick, and Sue, were over, and again Brian was answering for me when Derrick, who worked for social services, said to Brian, "You must stop always answering for Pat." Brian did not like the fact that he was doing anything wrong.

We did not stay in that house long; we sold it and moved into a better part of the neighborhood. It was a lovely home. We were not there long before we invited Derrick and sue over again. Brian said to them, "Have you ever thought about wife swapping?" Sue, who was Scandinavian, thought it a great idea. Brian took Sue by the hand without further ado and took her upstairs to our bedroom. I looked at Derrick and could not stop shaking, and Derrick said, "Don't worry, we will not be doing anything." Finally, it was happening; Brian wanted to be with other women; I always knew that he had been with other women before he met me and during the time we had been married. Did I think to myself, what marriage? This marriage is a sham.

One day Sue and Derrick were over, and Sue said that she had been speaking with her doctor, who she thought was exceptionally good looking, and told him about spouse swapping and would he like to get involved. He said yes, so Sue invited him over to our house. Sue was going with Brian and said I was to go with this man. Did I not have any say in this whole thing, with Brian and Sue telling me to do this and do that? I was not a happy person, and I did not like what was happening in my life, my marriage. Again, I thought, what marriage. The doctor drove me to this motel, and I had no idea what I was supposed to do. When the doctor said to me, "Get undressed." He was very authoritative, like Brian. I was scared, so I undressed. It was not very nice what he did to me. I felt so cheap, dirty, and disgusted.

One day, Brian and I were in town when he said, "I want to see you with other men." He said, "I have this magazine for spouse swapping, and I want us to get involved with other couples." By this time, I had started drinking to deal with what was happening in our lives. Under Brian's control, I was becoming significantly repressed. My boy's what about my boys! My precious sons, this is not right! How can this be happening?

Nevertheless, I had no say in it. I knew it was wrong, so unbelievably bad. What was I to do? I did not have a marriage anymore; did I ever have one, I wondered. David, If I had only given you a second chance, this would not be happening. I felt like I was living in hell. Little did I know that this would get worse. Brian would look up people in the magazine and get me to phone them and arrange a meeting. Then one day he saw this advert for a party in a penthouse in Winnipeg and wanted us to go there. By now, I was becoming numb to what was happening. I was not the same person; the person I used to be, was gone from me. I was becoming increasingly perverse; I felt like a dirty rag doll, down in the miry clay; I had lost sight of the person I used to be. Who am I? What is happening to me? We went to the party in Winnipeg, and there were people there all in a state of undress. There was a woman across from me that I at once took to; she was warm and quiet. So, when people went off with each other, I went with her. She was friendly and loving, and when a man came near me, I kicked him out of the way. It was her husband, but I wanted none of it. As the evening went on, she went with other partners, so I had no choice.

There is a lovely mall in Winnipeg called the City Place Shopping Centre. I have visited it at times. This one time, Brian drove the boys and me there, parked the car, and went inside. Suddenly he said to me; I am going across the road; there is a prostitute there who I would like to see and have that experience. I was no longer surprised at what Brian would say. The boys and I were to wait for him where we were so that he would not have to go looking for us. He had not been gone long when he returned and said she was not there. After that, we met a couple we became friends with and would see them every week and go to this place with them that was for swingers! Then it became masochism and sadism, spanked by somebody in control of you. It was getting worse. I did not like myself; I said to Brian, "no more" I cannot continue with this; it is destroying me; I do not like who I have become. "This is evil; why are you making me do this?" Then I received the silent treatment, and he would sit in his chair and sulk. It was just as hard to deal with the silent treatment, so I relented; however, I made sure I was drunk before we left to go to the swinger's club. Then one day going to this place, I became hysterical in the car and wanted to go back home, but he refused. Then I tried to kill myself, and I did not want to live anymore while I was with Brian.

Then our friends shared that they had gone to Jamaica and said what a terrific time they had there and that we should go. Therefore, we booked to go. I'm going to, I thought naively, restore our marriage, so I started fantasizing about our wonderful holiday. We arrived in Jamaica and went to our room; it was lovely. Brian said, "I will get changed and see you later." "What, aren't you going to wait for me?" "No, I will see you down there." Dismayed, I set about sorting out the clothes and changed, when a knock came at the door, I went and opened it, there was this Jamaican who pushed through the door, pushed me to the floor and raped me. Then he left as soon as he arrived. I was sick; why is this happening? I was heartbroken. After cleaning myself up, I decided to go down and find Brian. I saw him near the bars; he did not want me; he had all these other women lined up around him. What was I to do? I felt worthless, and all my hopes just fell to pieces. I went to the bar and got myself a drink. I met people there and talked to them and went off to a party in one of the rooms, where I met other people, we just talked and drank, later we all decided to go down to the beach. I went off with Jeff, who was from New York; we hit it off straight away, and for the rest of the holiday, I stayed with Jeff as Brian had taken one of the women to our room, so I could not go there. I had a wonderful time with Jeff, and it was truly romantic. We had arranged to stay connected at the end of the holiday, so had Brian with his date. I have never mentioned the rape to anybody till now.

Back in Canada, we stayed connected with our dates. I no longer wanted Brian to touch me. Something had happened to me that gave me a new strength that I had not had before. Jeff would phone me quite often, as I arranged to fly out to New York to see him, and at the same time, Brian would go to see his new women. I was changing, and I knew I could not go back to the way things were with Brian; the same went for him; he found what he wanted in this new woman. I finally told Brian that I wanted a divorce and would leave him. We had been married, if you can call it that, for fourteen years, the last eight years being in Canada.

I was working by now; however, my wage was not very much, and I knew I would not be able to support my sons as much as I wanted them with me; therefore, I agreed for Brian to have the boys if I could see them every weekend. He was not happy that I was leaving; nevertheless, I could not continue. I did not know what would become of Jeff; however, I knew I had to make this break. I went to see a social worker, as I needed someone to talk to about my sons. She asked me if I had told them what was going on in the marriage. I said, "I cannot tell them what was going on in the marriage; it is too horrible." After hearing what had been going on in the marriage, the social worker felt I should speak to them. I have not been able to do this. "The Lord willing, I pray this book will let them see the truth."

Eventually, I discovered that Jeff was not what he proclaimed to be; this hit me quite hard; I was very vulnerable and realized this, and I knew that I would have to make substantial changes. How? I asked myself, I was depressed and could not stop crying. I went to my doctor, who said you must have time off work and go on holiday for a couple of weeks, or I am going to put you into hospital. The divorce had gone through by this time, and I had received my half of the house sale. So, I arranged to have two weeks off work and go to Barbados, which I did. I love the Caribbean, as I love to swim, and the warm waters there; I find it very relaxing to swim in, plus the beautiful beaches. The time there evaporated all I had been through with Brian and Jeff. Unfortunately, when I went back to work after my holiday, I no longer had the job I had worked at for years, there was another woman now working at my desk. Realizing that I now had a different work to do was hard to deal with as my emotions were still taut, I decided to strive and get on with the new position.

Brian phoned me up one day at work to see if I wanted to go for lunch; I decided to go as I did not want to cause any waves between us in case, he made it difficult for me to see my sons. Our lunch was at a strip joint, and I was disgusted. I told him that I never wanted to go to that place again. Time went by, and Brian phoned and asked if I wanted to go for lunch. I suggested the restaurant across from where I worked. Sitting at the table and waiting for our meals, he was suddenly looking all-around at the women and girls. Brian suddenly said to me, "All those pussies, I want to eat them all." I was so disgusted at his depravity that I walked out.

I tried dating after a while, but this was not working out for me. I did not trust men; plus, I had a distaste for them. I became very depressed, and one day while having a Black Russian drink, I kept on drinking, one after another, and decided I did not want to face another day, so I decided to swallow a large bottle of Tylenol and went to bed thinking that was it. In the middle of the night, I suddenly awoke, not feeling well, and thought, what have I done? I called out; I do not want to die; I want to live! At this time in my life, I knew nothing of God or Jesus, but God, unbeknown to me, had his hand on me. The next day, I went to the doctor and told him what I had done. He scolded me and said if that were Aspirin, you would be dead; however, you are by no means out of the wars, and I will keep my eye on you for the next six months. From that time on, I did nothing but eat citrus and salads to help myself become healthier, and fitter, plus I rode my bike everywhere. I enrolled in Ballet classes as I still remember the movements from when I took ballet; this is a dance that I loved and will help me become fit. My life was changing, and there would be a new meaning to my life now. I was becoming free of my past.

CHAPTER 4

TIAMO

I had terrific friends at work, and these women were to have a substantial role in my life. Janice, one of my friends, knew I did not want to go out of a night-time, said to me, "There is going to be a fashion party, and we would like you to come along." I thought to myself, that sounds safe enough, little did I know what the night would bring. My friends arrived at my apartment to take me to the party. Which I immensely enjoyed. When it was time to leave the party and return home, we all seated ourselves in the car and left. Suddenly, I realized that we were not driving towards my home but away from it.

"I said, what is going on? Where are you taking me?" Janice said we are taking you to a nightclub, and you are going to have a night out with us." Reluctantly I agreed but said to them, "You are not to leave me on my own." Arriving at the nightclub, we all sat at the same table and ordered our drinks. After a while, we all went up to the dance floor. During the time on the dance floor, I noticed this man watching us; when we went back to our table, I walked by the man watching us when he spoke to me and said, "Would you have the next slow dance with me?" Without questioning him, I said, "Yes, I will." What was I thinking! I went and told the girls. The following slow dance was the Italian Love song, Tiamo; the man came up to me and said, "I am Paul, will you dance with me?" He was pleasant; we sat at a table near the girls after the dance. I did not want to lose sight of them. Paul and I talked. He seemed genuinely friendly. He wanted my phone number, but I refused and said you could have my work number and told him where I worked.

Paul phoned and asked if I would go out with him; I said, "No." He called me four times that week, each time I said, "No." On the weekend, I thought, am I being fair with Paul, could he be a decent man? So, I looked up his name in the phone book. A woman answered, I said, "Does Paul live there?" she replied, "Yes." I said, "Oh no, he's married; he's no different than the other men." "No, she answered, I am his sister. Paul came on the line, saying, "I'm not married; this is my sister, Grace." Relief flooded me, and we arranged to meet.

Paul and I dated for three years; I did not give him an easy time, as I had difficulty trusting him. Paul, however, was incredibly supportive of me. During this time, Paul arranged for me to see a psychiatrist as he knew how my so-called marriage to Brian had traumatized me. However, the psychiatrist did not help, talking about how the wild animals would mate. He was very odd. One day, I had a phone call from my uncle in England to tell me that my dad was dying of cancer and that it was aggressive, that they did not expect him to last much longer. I arranged with the doctor I worked for to have time to go to Ireland to see my dad. He would only give me a week off. I made the arrangements to fly to Ireland that week. My brother was driving mum to the airport to meet me and take me back home to dad. My poor dad had gone from a robust-looking man to this thin yellow-coloured shell of a man.

I ran to him and hugged him; it was awful; I thought my heart would break. Seeing my dad like that and realizing how he was suffering; was so hard to take in. My dear dad, I loved him and knew that I would be losing him soon. During my week with him, I would chat with him and try to soothe him. I had baby oil with me, so I would massage him to erase his skin's dryness and help ease the pain; how he loved me to do this for him. I started to tell him about Paul and our hopes for the future. He was so pleased for me. Because Paul was Italian, he would say to me about his time in Italy during the war how he loved Italian food and the people. He had opened about his time in the war for the first time. The week went too fast, and it was time to leave dad. Knowing that I would not be seeing my dad anymore was extremely painful for me. I was going to need Paul's support when I arrived back in Canada.

My brother drove me back to the airport to catch my plane back to Canada; saying our goodbyes; I boarded my plane to fly back to Canada. It seemed very strange knowing I would not see my dad again. I was not going to be able to receive letters from him anymore and knew that the connection that tied our family together would be gone. Oh, dad, I cried inwardly; I will miss you terribly.

The flight was just over seven hours and uneventful. Paul met me at the airport, and while driving me home, I told him about dad and how ill he was. I was grateful for the time I had with him, short as it was. However, I would not be seeing him ever again tore me in two. Yes, I was upset; I had loved my dad so much. I thought to myself, why did I not go back sooner to see him? I know that he and mum visited me in Canada when I was still with Brian. We had all travelled to stay in a chalet on a lake. Dad enjoyed himself so much, swimming and fishing. We were given a large Pike to grill on the barbecue, which he relished. In the evening, we would toast marshmallows and watch the Racoons looking at us from the tree, and then gradually, they would slowly approach and put their little hand out for a marshmallow. It was a joy to see; they were so very precious.

Coming out of my reverie on dad, I asked Paul what he had been up to while I was away? The revelation of what Paul next told me would be more than I could now bear. Paul had been out to a disco and met a girl he danced with and had spent time tother. Right away, I could see Brian over again, oh please, not Paul too, I thought as tears streamed down my face. When we arrived back at my apartment, Paul came in with my bags and put them down in the bedroom. Suddenly the dam burst inside of me, my dad and now Paul; I became hysterical and yelled at him, would I ever be able to trust him again. I tore off the necklace I had been given and threw it at him with such force that something broke on the dressing table.

I ran out of the apartment and jumped into my car, and drove, not knowing where I was going. I was tearing down the escarpment road, not caring if the vehicle went off the road. Suddenly, by some miracle, my car was in an alcove under the escarpment on the other side of the road; I sat there shaking. A driver in his car coming towards me asked if I was all right? I numbly said, "yes." When I had gathered myself together, not knowing what had happened or how I was on this side of the road, I drove down to the glen, switched off my engine, and cried and cried. Later, I felt the presence of a car next to mine, and it was a police car; the officer came and shone his torch at me and asked what was wrong? He could see that I had been crying; I relayed everything that had happened, about my dad, then Paul. He just sat and listened to me. Then after a while, he said, "I am going to escort you out of here; then, I want you to go home and have yourself a cup of tea." I thanked him for his help and promised him that I would take his advice. In the meantime, Paul had been out in his car searching for me. When Paul came to my apartment, he was at a loss, and he did not know what to say; he hugged me to him. The year was 1980, and dad passed away shortly after.

One day, at the apartment, I received a phone call from Brian, who asked me if I would go back to him? I said, "no." Then he said to me, "why would you want to go out with an Italian?" then he made a crude comment, so I hung up the phone on him. After that, he started giving me trouble about seeing the boys, sending me letters about the boys, saying things that were not true. One was so bad that I became hysterical. I loved my sons; I knew why Brian was doing this to me; I showed Paul the letter Brian had sent me. After reading the letter, Paul said, "I will have you see a lawyer and find out how you can get custody of your sons." However, this Paul did, due to their age, being fifteen and sixteen years old, they would be able to choose for themselves where they wanted to live. Eventually, they would take turns coming to stay with me, however, never permanently.

It was coming up to Christmas, and we had been dating for six months; I wanted Paul to have a special Christmas; I prepared a Christmas tree and set off to the mall to buy Paul's Christmas presents. I had so much fun doing this. Knowing that Paul would not be around till later, I wrapped up his presents and laid them under the Christmas tree. When Paul came in later, he said, "What are all those presents and who are they for?" I can still see him standing there, amazed, or should I say astonished. Paul came in carrying a load of parcels; I said, "What have you got there?"

"Ha! Ha!" he said, you will have to wait and see." We had such a lovely Christmas; my sons came and had their presents. Unfortunately, it did not matter what Paul did for them; they were not very friendly towards him. Due to their father's prejudice, I believed. Another time I remember, Paul's birthday was coming up, and I wanted to give him a surprise birthday party. I contacted his friends and asked them to say the word to his other friends. I had to be careful so that everyone arrived before Paul. I wanted to have everything ready for when he would come through the door. My friend Jill and Fred, her boyfriend, were going to be there; my son John wanted to be there, which pleased me. Everything worked out like clockwork, lights were out, and Paul drove up in his car. Then minutes later, he was opening the door, everyone shouted Surprise; Wow, was he surprised, shocked, and pleased, all simultaneously. It was a great evening; everyone enjoyed themselves.

By now, Paul and I had been dating for almost three years. I wanted to marry him, but I was scared; I still had a trust issue. Would I ever be able to trust anyone again? I thought to myself. Nevertheless, Paul was the love of my life, and I loved him with every being of my soul. We decided to set a date, and it was to be on the same month and date that we had met. Being Italian meant that the family was immense. My friends, the doctors I worked for, and their wives, plus girls from the office, were on my side. Paul and I wanted to arrange everything for the wedding ourselves so that it would be just as we would like it; however, Paul's mum and dad wanted to have the wedding reception catered by friends of theirs, which was fine, as Paul and I often went for a meal at their restaurant. Paul's sister was to be a bridesmaid, my close friend Jill was my Maid of Honour, and Jan, my friend, a bridesmaid. I had a tailor make the bridesmaid dresses, and I went with my friends to choose my gown. Unfortunately, having paid a down payment on the gown, the store, shortly after that, went bankrupt. I lost my money, so I had to look for another dress, which I did, and it was perfect; the gown was beautiful, far better than the first one. Then it was to bring Paul's mum to the store to choose a garment for the wedding. We found a lovely gown for her, and she looked beautiful in the outfit.

Paul's, mum, and dad were lovely people, and they became mum and dad to me. I loved them so much. Paul's family became my family, and it was terrific. I felt like I finally belonged. Paul's mum was such a loving, gentle lady; his dad was very caring and helpful. They were old-fashioned Italians, very warm and kind, so different from what I had experienced growing up. The extended families were, too, very loving and kind and welcomed me into the family.

The deposit for the Tuxedos for Paul, his dad, best man, and the ushers paid. We were to be married in the Lutheran church and met with the vicar, a genuinely lovely gentleman who took Paul and me through the preparation for our marriage. The hall for the reception booked, the Disk Jockey booked, and the music arranged, the limousines ordered, flowers ordered, invitations sent out, it was becoming extremely exciting as the event neared. Mum was flying over to Canada for the wedding, as she would be giving me away. Her brother and his wife had taken her out to buy a beautiful dress for the wedding.

The day of the wedding was a beautiful June day, knowing Paul and I were to be married and the day had finally arrived was breath-taking. The wedding service was very moving, and looking at Paul by my side, knowing we were to be husband and wife in the true sense, realizing how Paul and I loved each other was too marvellous for words. At the reception, our first dance was to be Tiamo, only this time, the Italian love song was our love song and would always be.

The first six months were heaven on earth; I was so in love with Paul, I could not believe a person could be so happy. However, as much as I loved Paul, things would never be quite the same again. Then one day, Paul came into our apartment, only this wasn't the same Paul, for some reason that I could not fathom, he was different. I said to him, "Paul, where have you been, and what's happened to you?" Paul replied that he had been to see a psychiatrist. I thought, what has happened? Paul said, "I have Paranoid Bi-Polar; the doctor has signed me off work for nine months. Starting a relationship with secrets is very unhealthy because it will come out. I had told Paul of my marriage, and Paul shared his Bipolar. Everything started to change. I never knew who would be coming through the door, Jekyll, or Hyde. Poor Paul, mental illness is not the person's fault who is suffering from it. I loved him dearly, and I was determined to support him and love him. Paul's attitude started to change, sometimes, he would be overly aggressive, and other times he would be loving; however, I knew it was the illness and not the person, plus the medication the doctor had him on would take time to level out his moods.

The year was 1987, and we had been married four years; we wanted to have our own home. Paul's mum and dad had two houses, their old home was next door to them, and they lived in a lovely bi-level home, with beautiful gardens around. They suggested we buy the old family home, and they would carry the mortgage. A family had rented the old house, and a man had rented the apartment accessed from the outside. The house was going to need renovation work done on it. Having taken interior decorating, I went in with a pad and pencil, and with the sketching, I could see that the house and the apartment could be lovely with new windows, decorating, and carpeting. The kitchen could be changed, with the sink near the window. Paul and I arranged for a kitchen company to come and design the kitchen for us. The old cupboards would go in the basement for storage. The bathroom would also need renovation and new plumbing installed, as with the kitchen.

I could envision what the house would look like, and I was excited by it all. I knew of a DIY man nearby and contacted him to see if he was available to do the work and, if he was, would he be willing to come and give an estimate for the job. I would take care of all the decorating and ordering of the carpets and flooring that we would need. Paul and I reviewed what the costs would be. The DIY man would order the windows for us. In the meantime, we would give notice at the apartment and rent a cottage across from our new home, making things so much easier for going back and forth from the work we would be doing on the house, as I was working all hours of the day and night to get it ready.,

One day during a phone call to my mother, mum had said how she needed to sell the family home and move into an apartment; however, they were all so expensive. We talked for a while then hung up the phone. Forgetting all that I had gone through with mum, I said to Paul, "What if mum comes over here to live, dad had longed to move over to Canada; he loved it here?" I said to Paul, "mum could have the apartment in the house; I could decorate it to look like a cottage." Paul said, "phone her back and ask if she would like to do that." So, I phoned mum back, and to cut a long story short, mum moved to Canada in 1987. How soon we forget the past!!

Paul and I were getting excited about mum arriving before Christmas. Paul and I went out and bought her all kinds of things she would need in her apartment. All her bedding and curtains to match her bedspread. Carpeting for the bathroom. It was everything that would lend itself to a cosy cottage. After completing the apartment, it indeed was lovely. The day arrived to go and pick up mum from the airport. Paul's mum and dad were very wary that my mum would be living in the apartment. They did not think it was clever to have mum so close to us. They were aware of the problems that I had in the past. Later in the week following mum's arrival to Canada, Paul and I took mum shopping for the furniture that she would need to move in after Christmas.

Before all this, I was at the local mall when I saw a van starting to move from its parking spot. On the van was the name of a regional breeding kennel of Golden Retrievers. I managed to stop the man driving the van to inquire where exactly the kennels were. I mentioned to him that my husband and I had bought a home and was wanting to have a Golden Retriever pup. I said, "would I be able to come to the kennels to see the dogs?" "Yes." He said, "anytime." Later that week, I visited the kennels; the dogs were beautiful, from golden to pale in colour. I met with the owner and asked if I could put my name down on the list for a dog. Paul and I were on the list, and I couldn't wait to tell Paul; he was thrilled.

Christmas day arrived, and Paul and I gave mum her presents for her apartment; she was thrilled. As Paul's family was coming for Christmas dinner, I had been baking we all had a lovely time. I loved Paul's family; I always felt comfortable around them; they were all genuine people. Over Christmas, I received a call from the breeder of Golden Retrievers to say, "Congratulations, your pup has just been born, oh what a lovely Christmas present, and she invited me to go there and see the puppies after Christmas. A contractor came and put up a fence around the garden and a gate affixed to it with a lock. In the new year, the house was ready, and it was even better than I had expected. Mum moved into her apartment, and Paul and I moved into the house. When the Retriever pup was seven weeks old, Paul and I went to collect her. We now had our new addition to our family, and her name was Sandy. Paul loved the little pup, and he would play with her for ages. We were thrilled to be in our new home for a while.

Mum started to cause trouble between Paul and me; she would yell at him, which did not help Paul or me. Mum made it clear that she did not like Paul. She expected Paul to be like dad, and they were as different as two peas in a pod. Why was mum causing us so much grief after all the things we had done for her? Paul and I had spent a lot of money on mum for her apartment; why wasn't she grateful? Didn't she realize? Why do we fantasize about how we would like things to be? I know I did with mum, visualizing her and me working in the garden together planting flowers. Did mum ever work in the garden back home? The answer was no; dad did everything. When I cleaned the oven (it was self-clean), I would open the windows during the cleaning process. Mum phoned down to me, yelling at me through the phone, "Are you trying to kill me?" "What's that smell?" More problems with mum.

With everything going on with mum affected Paul's Bipolar, he started to get into trouble with the police due to threatening people. One day, I asked my pastor from the Lutheran church where we were married and where I attended on a Sunday. Would the pastor visit me while Paul was at work? The pastor came over to the house, and I started telling him what was happening with Paul, when I received a phone call from one of Paul's workmates, telling me that the police were waiting for

Paul at his work Paul had gone to the house of one of the men and threatened his wife. Why was he doing this? I thought to myself, and then I relayed what was happening at Paul's work to the pastor. "Was it the Bipolar that he has that has caused all this? I was becoming distraught with all these violent episodes.

When Paul appeared before the judge, he was granted bail till the court hearing.

Paul did not use a lawyer at the court hearing but acted in his defence and won the case.

CHAPTER 5

THE ACCIDENT

January 1989 was a beautiful day for January, quite warm so that I did not have to wear a coat. Only this day I never reached home! I was driving home from work to let Sandy, my Retriever, out into the garden, then take her to mum's in her apartment and have lunch with her. My lights had changed to green, and cars were at the stoplights on my right, and there were no cars on my left, so I went ahead across the intersection when out of my eye I saw this car careening on to me; I just remembered screaming, when everything turned black. Next, I remembered gaining consciousness and in tremendous pain, wondering where I was and what had happened to me? Due to my head bouncing off my car window, I had sustained a brain injury that would leave me with horrendous headaches, unable to speak correctly, loss of memory, not of my family, though but of things that I should know. Severe back injury and unable to walk without the use of a stick.

Paul's family was there, and they had brought mum; however, Paul had not been made aware of my accident, his family refused to allow him to be called, in case he had an accident on the way from work to the hospital. Later that night, Paul would come in to see me. The doctor discharged me days later when he found out that the family was at home to look after me.

Paul was not there to bring me home; instead, he had arranged for a friend of his to go and pick up mum and get her to the hospital to bring me home. When being taken to the car to bring me home, my head and back pain was agony. I thought, will the pain ever stop. Then being helped inside my home to my bedroom, I was so relieved to be able to get into my bed. My Sandy was always there by my bed. She was to be my wonder dog, if I needed to go to the bathroom, which was across the hall from the bedroom, Sandy would take hold of the bottom of my dressing gown and help guide me, and with me holding on to my walking stick, we managed the two of us to get to the bathroom. She would sit and wait for me, then take me back to bed again. Sandy was to be my redeeming feature.

I have always loved to read; even from a young child, I would go off to bed at seven at night, get into bed and read a book until it was lights out. Now I picked up a book and started to read; however, I could not remember what the story was about as I turned the pages. I would think to myself, why can I not remember what I have read? Then I would realize that whatever anyone had said to me, the next instant, it would be gone from my memory. I wanted to make notes during this time but realized my ability to write, or print was gone. I had to relearn the alphabet. I thought if I can read, why can I not write? Something was missing. So, I started to try and copy sentences from the book I was reading, but my letters were not correct, so with the help of the alphabet, I would start to copy the letters down; sometimes they were good, other times they were not.

I knew that this would take time; nevertheless, I was determined. Paul bought me a tape recorder for me to read from the book to try and correct my speech. When will I be normal again? What is normality? Are we ever the way we should be? The intense pain in my head, back, and body had become worse. The Neurologist had put me on strong medication for the pain, but it still wasn't working, so I was given even more potent medicines; this started to help; it made things manageable. Thinking to myself, I will overcome all of this, and I will get better again, then I said to myself, you are an achiever. I hung on to this through the months that followed. I found out that nerve damage in my hand and arms was causing me problems writing correctly; however, I would not give up. I would use the tape recorder that Paul had given me to read and re-read a book aloud, listening to how I sounded. After months of doing this, my speech started to sound more fluent.

Back and forth to the doctors and Neurologist, it was highly frustrating. Still, these excursions also severely affected me, having to try and go over the accident, the different doctors asking questions that I found difficult to answer. One Neurologist at a medical university had me do assessments to see what my cognitive functions were due to the bruising of my brain. After the test, he told me that I would never be academic again or be able to go out to work, plus I would have to avoid stress in my life as this would harm my health. His words hit me hard; I said to myself, I will prove you wrong and go out to work again. Back at home, I would work on copying words down and practicing capital letters and small letters; I wanted a writing pattern. Gradually, the letters started to get better, and then I began to copy out sentences from a book. It was not perfect, but it was a significant improvement; I was determined to keep at it until my writing started to flow. I will succeed, I thought to myself, that doctor is not going to tell me that I will not work again. I will prove him wrong. Now, what am I going to do about my memory? I said, to Paul, "I cannot seem to remember things you have told me." Paul said, why don't you start writing down things told to you." After much effort and discipline, plus tears of frustration.

Nevertheless, slowly, I started to remember enough to get by overtime. It had been ten months since the accident. I know it was very frustrating for Paul. However, he knew the accident settlement would bring in big money and saw the dollar signs. There were so many visits to the lawyers, counselling, and visits to the doctors for the insurance company. More visits to other Neurologists with more tests became utterly overwhelming. For most of the year, we would be going back and forth.

Paul took me to buy another car, as the person who drove into me had wrecked my car in the accident. My counsellor had to take me out in the car to help me relax while driving as every time I came to the green light; I would draw to a stop, I was afraid to continue. All this took time as I had lost my confidence in driving. In December 1989, I was sure that I would work again. Neurologist's advice about not working again, his words still echoed in my ears, "You will never be academic again; you will have to get used to the idea of staying at home." I was determined to prove him wrong. I will fight this and go back to work again, and no one will stop me. I will prove to them that I can work. How am I going to do this? I thought to myself. I need to do something to help my memory, and I need to take control of my speech and be able to write correctly. This thought kept running through my mind. I will do this, and I will succeed. I had come a long way; however, I still had a long haul, but I will do it.

One day, while scanning the newspaper for a job opportunity, there was an advertisement for a seminar at one of the motels in town for work in the insurance field. I thought about this and felt a surge of excitement swell up in me. I would go along. The seminar was fascinating, and I thought this was something I would like to do. My speech was good, plus I would work on it more. My writing had come along, although I would have to work at this. I remembered nothing about grammar, punctuation, and the rest for writing correctly; this would be a continuous learning lesson throughout my life. My memory still was not good. I knew this would be something that I would be continually working on; however, I would try to conquer this to the best of my ability. I phoned the insurance company and asked for an interview, which the manager gave me the next day. When I went for the interview, I did not hold anything back. I told the manager about my head injury and that I had a problem with my memory; nevertheless, I told him I was willing to learn. The manager said that I would have to pass an exam before I could start but that they would collaborate with me and give me all the help I needed. I was thrilled. The manager gave me books to study at home, and when I was ready, he would give me an evaluation to see how I was doing. He did this, and when he felt I was ready, he enrolled me to sit the exam. I failed the first time, almost passed the second time. Unfortunately, the manager said, I would have to wait another six months to sit the exam again. Then I said to the manager, "What if I wrote a letter to the insurance board and told them of my head injury and asked them if I could be allowed to sit the exams again?" The manager agreed to this, so I wrote a letter to the board, explaining my accident and head injury, asking them to allow me to sit the exams again, instead of waiting the six months. The manager sent the letter off, and within a week, The board sent a new exam date. I felt good the day I sat my exams, believing that I would pass this time. The results returned to the manager that

I had passed the exams, and I was thrilled. The last thirteen months had been long and hard, and finally, I felt that I had overcome all odds.

The work was enjoyable, and I excelled in it. I started to earn money, and it was mind-boggling to me, the amount of money I was making; however, it was long hours from early morning to late at night, sometimes near midnight. New strength and enthusiasm were developing in me. Had I overcome all odds, or was I losing sight of something more precious to me? Was I wrong in not harkening to the advice of the Neurologist? I was about to find out in the following months.

CHAPTER 6

TURMOIL

Paul and I would go to his mum and dad for supper every Thursday, which I loved. Also, I loved them a great deal, and they had been wonderful to me during my months of being laid up; I was so grateful to them. While at supper, I said where I had to go for insurance business that night. Paul's dad said, "You shouldn't be driving around at night-time; it is not safe; there was a car-jacking up at the lights." So, with that in mind, when I went out that night, I was careful to lock my car doors while driving around. This night would take me to a home in an unsavoury part of Winnipeg. The numbers on the houses were not noticeably precise, so I parked my car and started to walk up the street. Suddenly this Shepherd dog was beside me, then disappearing, then back again. When I arrived at the house, the dog was with me; the woman answering the door said I must ring the humane society about that dog. I was with her for about two hours, taking care of her insurance. When I came back out, the dog was waiting for me. Again, he disappeared, as I walked back towards my car, which was a two-door sedan, opening my door, I climbed into the car, and I suddenly felt a presence in the car, I looked behind me, and there was the Shepherd dog on my backseat. I never knew how he could have gotten into the car to this day. I said to the dog, "Hello, are you coming for a ride with me?" I thought to myself; I would drive down to my office and phone the Humane Society to find out if anyone had lost this dog. There was no dog record, so the man at the society said: "If you give us your address, we will pick the dog up tomorrow for you." I said, "Thank you," and hung up the phone; this dog would get a new home. Arriving at home that night, Paul was leaving for his night shift, and I told him what had happened; Paul was thrilled; the dog's name was going to be Mickey. Paul left for work, and I walked with Mickey around to our garden, opened the gate, and let him in. Not wanting to bring a strange dog into the house with Sandy, I let Sandy out into the garden to meet Mickey. It was the weirdest thing; you would have thought that they already knew each other how they were running around the garden together, then coming together into the house. Not knowing the dog's personality, I thought I would let him sleep in the basement. When I opened the basement door, and Mickey saw the stairs, never in my life have I seen fear, as I saw in his eyes; therefore, I closed the door, gave him a brush and something to eat and drink.

Sandy had already gone to bed and was asleep. I thought to myself, I will see what Mickey does. I readied myself for bed and climbed in, Mickey came and laid by the side of my bed, and when I awoke the following day, he was still asleep in the same place. I noticed Mickey was very thin, so I knew that Mickey would need building up. However, when he laid down and stood up, I noticed that he was wincing. So, I phoned the vets to see if I could bring him in for a check-up. At the vets, the Vet noticed that Mickey had an injury to his hip; after having an x-ray the following day, the Vet informed me that Mickey had Hip-Dysplasia.

With special supplements, I would be able to help him. Well, now I had two dogs with Hip-Dysplasia; Sandy previously had been diagnosed with this. Now, Sandy and Mickey will be on Cod Liver Oil. I will take care of this precious dog. Now, when I go out of a night-time, Mickey would be accompanying me; he would be my bodyguard, how he loved to travel around with me. I could not take Sandy, as someone might try and steal her, but they would think twice with Mickey before trying to come near him. When walking them one day, I found out that two men were coming towards us, and Mickey let out a low growl as a warning to them.

I was still suffering from back pain and headaches, and I went to see a therapist that I would visit regularly. The therapy helped at the time; however, it would not last; I was in constant pain. Nevertheless, I was determined not to let the pain affect my work. I was becoming successful at what I was doing, and the insurance company had encouraged me to take the car and home insurance exams; this I did and sailed through the exams, to my immense joy. I enjoyed these products even more than the regular life insurance; it was more involved, and I relished it.

Mother's Day was coming up, and I wanted to get a companion for mum to keep her company. I had seen an advert in the paper about a breeder of Bichon Fris who had pups ready to go to a new home. I spoke to Paul about getting mum a puppy for herself, and he thought this a clever idea. I phoned the breeder and arranged to see the dogs, this I did, the pups were so cute, I arranged with her to come back later, after I had bought all the necessary things mum would need, such as puppy food, collar, and leash, brush. The puppy was so cute, a little bundle of white fur. I arrived home, pulled into the garage, and opened the garden door from the garage; Paul was waiting; I went into the garden and called up to mum, asking her if she would come down. She did, and when she was in the garden, I said, "Close your eyes and put your hands out," when she had done this, I placed the pup in her hands. A look of joy went on her face as she saw the puppy. I said, "Happy Mother's Day," She looked at the pup and said, "I will call him Benji." A new love relationship between mum and the puppy. She loved him, and how my dogs loved him, especially Mickey; this little dog could do anything with Mickey and became great pals.

Paul was incredibly good at taking me to see other doctors; nevertheless, our life at home was not so good. I would always be home to cook dinner, usually three courses. However, before I had completed my meal, Paul had finished and was up from the table saying, "I am going to take a shower, as I am going out. This happened every night, and he would shower and get dressed up and go out, never saying where he was going, and would most often arrive home between 2 am and 4 am—never saying where he had been. Paul and I were drifting apart, so I spoke to him and suggested we have a lunch date once a week. Unfortunately, that did not help; sitting at the table in the restaurant felt like sitting with a stranger; worse than that, I felt alienated from him. It became extremely uncomfortable. Then the threatening started, and Paul started to become violent towards me. Then six months into my job, things became intolerable at home. Paul would start threatening me and saying, "You wouldn't dare leave me." Sneering at me as he said this. He had been talking about the Mafia for a while now, which was prevalent in parts of Winnipeg. I had never taken him seriously, but now I was beginning to wonder what was going on? I knew there was the Italian, Sicilian, and Russian Mafia. I knew where some of them hung out and avoided those areas.

Paul had not wanted to be with me to make love for quite a while now; even though I had bought beautiful nightwear to entice him, nothing seemed to work. I would go to bed in tears and cuddle up with Sandy and Mickey. I heard people in the neighborhood were talking about seeing Paul with other men. I thought to myself, is this why he does not want me anymore? Paul threatening me was increasing, the stress was getting so bad that I just could not deal with it, I was becoming sick again, the pains were far worse than they had been. So, I went to see the lawyer I had for my accident. Ted said, "I will send you upstairs to a woman lawyer who will advise you what to do." Ted phoned the lawyer, who told Ted that she would see me. Jill was her name, and she was genuinely friendly; I felt comfortable with her and went ahead to tell her what had been happening between Paul and myself and the way he had been threatening me, his going with other men. Then I told her of Paul's income and him taking out loans with both our names on them. Where was all the money going? I recently noticed that Paul had all kinds of credit cards, for what? I told Jill that I was becoming more scared of Paul during our conversation. Where was the man I had married? We had been married for seven years, yes, I still loved him, but now, I feared him. Jill recommended that I move out of the house, "Do you have anyone to help you?" she asked me. "Yes, I could ask my sons if they would help." Then Jill said, "I will get the separation papers drawn up for you." I phoned John, my eldest son, to see if he and Ken would help me. We arranged that they would come down with a U-Haul truck on Saturday morning. While Paul was out for the night, I started sorting and packing what I would need. I had not thought about where I would live!

Paul always went out for breakfast on Saturdays and usually came home around lunchtime. Therefore, he was out when my sons arrived with their girlfriends to help me pack. I was going to take half of the furniture and leave the rest for Paul. Unfortunately, Paul came back early and went into the house and asked me what was happening. I was crying and said to Paul that I was leaving him and could no longer deal with what was happening in our lives. Paul was the love of my life; however, I knew I had to leave him. Paul went around to tell his mum and dad. I had nowhere to go, so I phoned a real estate person to ask if he knew of any apartments available where I could go, explaining that I needed to get out of my home that day. He asked me to go and meet him, and he would see what he could do. I met him at his office, taking my check book with me, and I knew I looked like a mess; however, I could not help that. The agent said that he had phoned a couple of men he knew and that they had an empty apartment that I could move in that day. Meeting with the two men, I arranged to move in that day. I paid them a month's rent, and they gave me a key. The apartment was not in the best part of town; however, I had somewhere to live and be with my dogs, Sandy and Mickey.

Driving back home to help my sons, I met with chaos. Paul's mum and dad were there and started accusing me of leaving their son, who was sick. They did not care that I was unwell too and on the verge of a nervous breakdown. It was awful because I had loved them so much. The row with them, the way they were attacking me, was too much, and I became hysterical. I couldn't calm down and had to tell my mum that I would be in touch with her. My sons and their girlfriends helped me move into the apartment with Sandy and Mickey. I was safe for a while, or was I?

CHAPTER 7

MISERY

One day coming in from work, there was a message on my phone from Paul. Oh, the horror of it, the statement said, "I know where you are, I will get you, you pig." I took the tape out of the recording, went down to the police station, and made a report. In the room with the officer, I felt like I was the guilty one; he made me feel very uneasy. However, he said he would bring Paul in for questioning and would keep an eye on the place where I lived. I knew I had to get out of the place where I was living, so I started to scan the newspaper for a place where I would feel safe. There was a house for rent in Minnedosa. I phoned mum and asked her if she wanted to move out of the apartment and come and live with me in Minnedosa, she said that she would, so I told her, "We could split the rent between us." I will plan to go and view the house and call you back. The people who owned the house had just finished building it. The home was a bungalow backing onto fields in a small urban setting. There were three bedrooms; therefore, Mum could have a bedroom and a sitting room if she wanted to be on her own. The bungalow had a lovely porch in the front, and at the back was a deck off the kitchen and steps to the garden. It was quite lovely. Therefore, I arranged payments for each month. Mom and I moved in together. Jill and Fred helped mum and moved her furniture for her to the home, and my sons helped move me into the home along with Sandy and Mickey, plus they had their playmate, Benji. They had a lovely big garden to play in, plus there were lovely walks to go on here in Minnedosa. Mum and I settled into our new home. All was well, or was it?

I had left my first job in Winnipeg and had a new job with another insurance company close to Minnedosa. At first, it was great, and I liked the people I worked with; However, things were not so great at home! Mum would be drinking throughout the day and shout at me when I arrived home from work, saying she was not my skivvy. What was she saying? In the beginning, mum would get a start on dinner for me, but now she just wanted to sit and watch the TV with her glass of brandy. Therefore, I would prepare and cook dinner for us. I did not wish to have any arguments with her. Mum had her sitting room and a separate bedroom. Which was good; nevertheless, mum was getting bad-tempered again. One day, I went out to my car and saw that all my tires had been slashed. Who could have done this? I phoned the police and reported the incident. Thankfully, my car insurance would cover this. After the police had inspected the damage, I arranged for a tow truck to tow my car into the nearby town to get the tires replaced. Was this Paul's doing? We had observed him and his family driving down the road where we lived. The police were going to have Paul in again for questioning.

One of my clients in Minnedosa mentioned that a lovely bungalow further into the village was for rent, plus the rent was lower than what mum and I were paying, plus there was a locked garage joined on to the place. I went to have a look at it. This place had a lovely large garden and beautiful old trees. Not only that, but the basement was carpeted throughout so that the house would be warmer.

It was a dream bungalow; I fell in love with it. I arranged to meet with the owners, they were friendly people, and we could arrange a time for mum and me to come and live in the house. It was going to need decorating inside, which I would be able to do. The home also had three bedrooms, so mum would still have a bedroom and a sitting room, which was good. Now to go home and tell mum that we would be moving further into the village, this would be better for both of us. This house, too, backed onto fields.

When I told mum, she yelled and screamed at me that she was not moving. I went to a mutual friend to see if they could help persuade her and let her know that it would be much more beneficial for us to move into the new bungalow. The garage would give us more security, and Paul would not likely find us there in the new place. The garden would be even better for the dogs; it was a lovely big garden with patio doors. We moved into the new bungalow; it was charming and cosier than the first bungalow; it was more of a home. However, there was a strain between mum and me. Plus, I was getting incredibly stressed out and having a challenging time with my job. It was becoming exceedingly difficult for me to do the work. I realized that I could not do the work; something had happened to me. One day driving into work, I did not know where I was; I stopped the car and looked around; I felt very strange, not controlling myself. I thought, what if I start going back the way I had come? I could find my way home. I eventually did this; upon reaching home, I phoned the doctor and told him what had happened. The doctor said I want to see you in my office today. I managed to reach the doctor's office, and upon seeing him and talking to him, he said to me, "You have had a mental breakdown; I am signing you off of work for six months." What would I do? Where would the money come from to pay the bills? Finally, I met with trustees to discuss if I should claim bankruptcy. They were accommodating; they knew about Paul and that I was fearful of meeting him. They said that they would look after me. So, I became bankrupt, and everything ceased. It was an awful time. I did receive a long-term disability payment that had been long overdue, which helped mum and me out for a while.

My son Ken was to be married and had invited my uncle and cousin to their wedding. They would be flying over from England for the wedding. Then, my uncle, cousin, mum, and I were to be traveling up to the lakes in Winnipeg, which would be fantastic. Ken and Celia had asked me to make the favour's for the wedding table, which took quite a while to do as three hundred guests were going to the wedding. I had taken mum out to buy an outfit for the wedding. We found a beautiful dress for her, shoes, and a purse to match. I had bought myself a two-piece suit and shoes and a bag to match. I went to help Celia get her makeup done for the wedding then it was time to go. Celia looked lovely; she had got into the car with her father and were off to the church. I was so pleased that I had my uncle and cousin at the wedding with mum and me. After the reception, it was time to leave to go back home and get ready for the holiday.

The holiday was fun; we travelled quite a long way, stopping in a restaurant on the way for a meal, then just before dark, we arrived at our destination. Chalets were scattered around, and there was a restaurant by the lake. Following dinner, my cousin and I sat by the lake, listening to the night sounds and the howl of the wolves high up in the hills. The next day we swam in the water, took canoes out, then in the afternoon, my uncle rented this giant skimmer that shot along the water; we wanted to see how far we could go. Unfortunately, it ran out of gas, my uncle was not incredibly happy with the owner, sending us out without enough fuel. My uncle said to stay with the boat and that he would follow the water edge back to the base and get help. Eventually, support came, and I can imagine he gave the owner a good telling-off. Mum was her usual self; her brother ignored her nonsense. We did a great deal of driving around, and it was great fun being with my uncle and cousin.

When I lived in Minnedosa, I met Allen, who worked in the town for a real estate company, and we had become friends. I knew I would not be able to stay in the bungalow, having claimed bankruptcy, plus I would not have the money for the rent and the utility bills. So, I said to Allen. "I will need to find something much cheaper to live and find mum somewhere to live where she would be happier." I spoke to mum and said, "Would you like to move into a senior's apartment building near the shops for you, where you can come out of the building, and there would be all kinds of shops to go to?" "Shall I look into this for you?" Mum agreed. Fortunately, there were apartments available for mum to move in. I asked Jill and Fred if it would be possible for them to help mum move into her new apartment. Jill and Fred took care of Mum's move. Mum settled into her new apartment. She was at the back of a small-town centre, plus there were lovely walks to take Benji on, and mum became more contented; she never liked the country setting; she was more of a town/city person. Here is where we differed so much. I have always loved the quiet of the countryside. Allen also found an apartment on an estate that we could rent; we decided to go in together to help each other out. It was a lovely apartment, very spacious on extensive grounds, with room to take the dogs for a run. We had fun there, entertaining, baking bread, and cooking up all sorts of good things to eat. The following month, we travelled up to his cottage with his two girls and my two dogs and had fun on the lake. I was still not sure that Allen was right for me. Time would tell.

Life at the apartment on the estate was good. The estate belonged to a doctor of Persian descent and was genuinely lovely. Inside his vast mansion were all these beautiful Persian carpets and Persian tapestries, I had never seen anything like this before, and I wondered at the magnificent splendour of what I saw. We had often sat and talked, there was one thing that I disagreed upon, and that was that he had these two beautiful Alsatians on a chain, one at each side of his main door to keep watch. I had met his sister, who often came to visit with him, and we had walked and talked together as we walked over the estate. I learned to use Olive Oil on the skin to keep it moisturized; this I still do; it is an excellent moisturizer and so much cheaper than regular skincare oils.

One day I saw the doctor outside, in great distress; one of his dogs was missing. The other dog was crying for its mate. When the doctor finally found his dog, the dog had fallen over the embankment and was covered in lice. I knew the dog would be in shock, and I was horrified when I saw the doctor putting the hose on the dog to try and get rid of the lice. I said to him, "I will phone my vet to see if he will help." The vet said he would, so I gave him the directions for the estate, and the vet arrived. By this time, the dog was suffering quite badly, so the vet said he would take the dog back to his surgery. Unfortunately, what the dog had experienced, brought about its death. I was so upset with the treatment that the dog had suffered; it was so wrong, which affected me badly; plus, the other dog knew he had lost its mate, the poor dog was mourning so pitifully, they had been together for years.

Mickey and Sandy loved the long walks around the estate; it was quite beautiful, with large old trees and lovely gardens. The estate and buildings were incredibly old. I enjoyed living there. However, I was not happy that I was living with Allen. Our relationship seemed very wrong. There was a lady pastor that I phoned and invited her to breakfast and a talk with me. The pastor was lovely, so I opened to her about my history with Brian and then Paul and the situation I now found myself in with Allen, saying to her, I wouldn't say I like living like this; it feels very wrong. Therefore, we discussed what turn of events should occur in my life. Even though I did not know the Lord Jesus yet, I was uncomfortable with my situation; it felt wrong somehow. The pastor agreed and suggested that I live on my own with my dogs. Then I knew that I had to decide about Allen, and because we were sharing the apartment, he should sleep downstairs in his bed. I was thanking the pastor for coming around and helping me. I put Allen's bed together in the lower bedroom and arranged all his belongings there. Unfortunately, when Allen came in later, he wanted to know what was happening.

I said to him, "I do not want us to sleep together anymore; it does not feel right to me and explained about my meeting with the lady pastor." Allen was furious that I did not want to sleep with him anymore. I said to him, "I cannot deal with this anymore." And fled from him up to the bathroom; next, Allen flings the door open to challenge me; in desperation, I slapped him around the face. I could not deal with it anymore in my life. The next day, Allen moved out of the apartment. Now, I thought to myself, how am I going to be able to pay the rent on my own? I met with the doctor's sister again and told her of the situation; now Allen is gone; she said to me, "You like gardening, don't you? I said, "Yes, I do."

Therefore, she said to me, "How would you like to take care of the gardens on the estate?" I said, "That would be wonderful." Then she said, "Do you think you could drive a lawnmower?" "Yes," I said. I now had a new job and money for the rent.

However, this job would play havoc with my back and head injuries, and eventually, I had to stop. I was having a tough time dealing with the pain in my back and head.

CHAPTER 8

HARDSHIP AND NEW BEGINNINGS

Three years since my accident, I was suffering again from a nervous breakdown. Having tried to work in the insurance field and then failing at my last job with insurance and investments, trying to cope, and not having the capabilities to do the work given to me. My marriage collapses, then later divorce, and the bankruptcy is on top of everything. Now, not being able to do the job on the estate, my nervous system completely broke down. Life was becoming hard to manage, and I did not know what to do or where to turn.

I was in bed, wracked with continual pain in my head and back, crying into the pillow. As I looked towards my books on my bedroom shelf, my eye caught hold of a book; slowly getting out of bed, I went and picked up the book; it was my old school, Bible. Suddenly a need surged through me; getting back into bed, I opened the Bible, and there before me was Psalm 23 that called to me. The Lord is my Shepherd; I shall not want. He maketh me to lie down in green pastures: He leadeth me beside the still waters. He restoreth my soul: He leadeth me in the paths of righteousness for His name's sake. Yes, though I walk through the valley of the shadow of death, I will fear no evil: for thou art with me: thy rod and staff they comfort me. Thou preparest a table before me in the presence of my enemies: Thou anointed my head with oil; my cup runneth over. Surely goodness and mercy shall follow me all the days of my life: and I will dwell in the house of the Lord forever. As I read the Psalm, tears ran down my face. Then read it repeatedly again, seeing the Lord holding my hand as He led through the Psalm. Laying me down gently on the green pastures, then leading me beside the still waters. How soothing was this to my heart and soul?

In January, six months later, having obtained work in an office of a large nursery in town. I had gone in for the interview with my resume that I had prior to my accident. I still refused to believe what the Neurologist had told me, about me not ever going out to work again. It was a challenge to me, and I desperately wanted to prove the doctor wrong. I was still fighting this.

Similarly, I tried to overcome my inability to do the job I was assigned to do. Was I scared? Yes, I could not understand why I could not do the tasks given to me? The nursery owner, I was to find out, was the President of the Full Gospel Businessmen's Fellowship International (FGBMFI), who asked me if I would like to type out the schedules of the upcoming speakers for the monthly meetings, this would include their testimonies. I was pleased to do this, and gradually over time, the testimonies started to affect me, and I asked if I could go to these meetings. The owner was thrilled, as no one from the office had ever wondered if they could attend the meetings. The owner arranged that I would go the following Monday and that I should sit at his family's table. Walking into the hall for the meeting the following Monday night, little did I know how different my life would be from that time on.

That night would be the beginning of a long journey I would take with the Lord Jesus Christ. The night of the meeting, I was moved by the testimonies given by the men. The hymns that people were singing. Impressed by what Jesus had done in the lives of these men, how they had given their lives to the Lord Jesus Christ and were now working on His behalf, giving back to Him with thanksgiving the new life that they now lived. As the evening ended, the President invited people to go forward to accept Jesus into their lives. As I sat in my chair, something was happening; I got up and went forward. As I reached the front, the President asked me if I wanted to accept Jesus into my life? Suddenly, tears started streaming down my face, and I knew without a doubt, "Yes," I wanted Jesus to come in and take over my heart and be in control of my life.

Now, as I walked out of that meeting, I knew that I was no longer the same person who had walked into the meeting earlier in the evening. Something so wonderful had changed in my life, I felt lighter, and I felt happy for the first time in years. I was at peace, but I was also experiencing perfect joy, knowing that I was no longer alone, and Jesus loved me for myself. I had Jesus in my life from then on. The glorious wonder of it all, that Jesus could love me a sinner, who had been down in the gutter in filthy rags, loved me. As I drove home, the hymns and worship songs came to me that we had been singing that evening, and I sang all the way home. Arriving home, I greeted my dogs with joy. Letting them have a run outside, the dogs and I then went up to bed. Sitting in bed that night, I opened my Bible up to Matthew, and an understanding was coming to me of what I was reading; the Holy Spirit was giving me a sense of what I read. I was so hungry for the Word of God and holding on to every word that I read. Finally, I put the

Bible down at three in the morning. I went peacefully to sleep. The next day at work, I could not keep a smile off my face; I was delighted.

I found out where the Full Gospel Church was and that Sunday, I was there to attend, and the following Sundays to come. I wanted to learn all that I could and get involved in Bible Study. While walking my dogs that night, a song came to me about the Lord, my Abba Father. I was so hungry for the Word of God. When I arrived home with my dogs, I took out my tape recorder and started to sing into it the words that the Lord was feeding me. Afterward, I played it back and wrote down on a pad all the song's words. Then I went and phoned the pastor and told him what the Lord had given me. He said, "The Lord has just given you your testimony." The wonder: of it all was the first of many songs the Lord would give me. I felt so blessed at what was happening in my life.

CHAPTER 9

THE BEGINNING OF FAITH

Two weeks later, at work, the manager, who reminded me of my Personnel Officer in my first job, gave me a letter, saying that they were not going to renew my contract and that I would have to leave in two weeks. I should have known this would happen; nevertheless, I was devastated; how would I pay my rent? Arriving at home that night, I collapsed in tears on the kitchen floor, crying to the Lord for help. Suddenly a feeling of a warm blanket covered me, then, a still small voice, saying, "You must write out your testimony and give a copy tomorrow at work, 1 copy to the owner and a copy to the manager." "Oh, how am I going to do this, I cried?" The still small voice said, "I will help you." Sitting down on my couch with pad and pencil, I started to write, yet it was not me writing; the words were flowing from the pencil to the pad through the help of the Holy Spirit. I could hardly believe what had just happened. My life up to that time was now on sheets of paper. I realized that the Lord was now in charge of my life. Not knowing where this was going to lead, I felt encouraged by this event and would start to lean on the Everlasting Arm of the Lord Jesus Christ.

The next day at work, I showed my obedience to the Lord, and feeling flustered, I went into the owner's office, saying that the Lord had directed me to do this. I did the same with the manager; they each understood that this direction had come from the Lord. By being obedient to the directions of the Holy Spirit, I now started my journey of faith. This total surrender to the Lord resulted in the manager and owner giving me two months to look for a job instead of two weeks. "Praise the Lord." During the last two months of my work, I did not go in this Wednesday; I was in so much pain with my back. As I was resting, the phone rang; upon answering it, I was shocked to find it was Paul on the phone.

I said, "How did you know where I was?" Paul answered and said, "I asked the operator for your number." Still shocked, I prayed quickly and realized this had to be the Lord's intervention, as I usually would not have been home. I related to Paul about receiving the Lord Jesus Christ into my heart and what the Lord had been doing for me. I told him about the monthly meetings on Mondays that I go to at the FGBMFI. Paul said, "I would like to go to one of those meetings," so I told him when the next meeting would be and where the hall was; the meeting was going to be the following Monday. I then asked Paul how he was? Paul said he missed the dogs. Again, I lifted a prayer to the Lord and said, "Would you like to meet the dogs and me at the park on Saturday?" Paul said, "He would." We arranged a time to meet on Saturday.

Next Saturday, I met Paul with my dogs, Sandy, and Mickey, having decided to share what I knew about Jesus Christ, my Lord, and Saviour. I attended the Full Gospel Church since accepting Jesus into my life. I was so hungry for the Word of God and what it meant to me in my life. I knew I still loved Paul, even after all that had happened; Paul was my first love, and that kind of love never dies. I was determined to reach Paul for Jesus. I realized that the Lord had His plans for Paul; it was up to Paul whether he would surrender his life to Jesus. A person cannot be forced; this has to come from a willing heart. Not everyone is ready to submit themselves to the Lord Jesus Christ. Paul and I spent an hour walking the dogs, and then Paul left promising that he would meet me on Monday at the FGBMFI meeting.

Paul did meet me that Monday; he was waiting for me to arrive. He enjoyed the meeting; it would take time for Paul to accept the Lord into his life. Paul was Catholic and would not do anything against what his parents wanted for him, except that they never knew that Paul and I met to walk the dogs each Saturday and that we would continue to do so for quite a while to come. During this time, Paul had bought himself a Bible. I had hoped that we would be able to study together; however, that never happened. Paul would only give me an hour each Saturday.

The men from the FGBMFI wanted to meet with Paul for a coffee and a talk, to be able to help him and reach him for Jesus. When one of the men phoned Paul's home where he was living with his parents, Paul's mum answered the phone and wanted to know what they wanted with her son. When they said they wanted to go for a coffee with Paul, she got angry with them. Paul would never call them back. He would not do anything to go against his parent's wishes, except to see me!

I was offered the post at a surgeon's practice as his receptionist. This job again was different from what I had experienced before. However, the doctor was very patient with me and showed me what I needed to do and how to fill in the forms for the various surgeries he had performed. Over time, I became more confident in what I was doing and quite liked the job. The patients were a joy to chat with, and I became known to them. During this time, I found a summer cottage to rent, which was half the price of what I was paying on the estate. The men from my church used trucks and said that they would move my furniture for me into the cottage. They did, and to thank them, I fed them a pot pie, which consisted of mixed vegetables and chicken. They loved it. I asked them if they would like pie for dessert, they all agreed that they would. I cut open the pie, which should have been a fruit pie, and to my horror, it was another pot pie; they laughed and said they would enjoy another pot pie instead of a fruit pie. The cottage was on the grounds of a farm, and fields were all around where I could walk the dogs. So, it all worked out well.

Unknown to me, and for me not to have the wherewith of understanding of summer cottages. Although the name, summer cottage, should have told me. There was no insulation whatsoever in the cottage. Even the walls would move in the wind. Winter in Manitoba is bitter, and the cold is extreme. Even my dogs, Sandy, and Mickey, did not like lying on the thin carpet on the floor with ice underneath it, which would crunch when I walked over the carpet. It was so cold there that everything froze up in the house one day. There was no water, as the pipes had frozen up. I was four days without water; it was no fun. I had the oven on and opened to try and get heat. The wall heater in the living room gave hardly any heat out. The only place we could be warm was upstairs in bed, curling up together. I would lay in bed and listen to the rats and mice running in the walls. One day, Mickey was in the other bedroom across from mine and was playing with something; I went over to investigate; I was unsure if it was a large mouse or small rat; it was dead. Oh, what am I to do? I do not like this; I grabbed it by the tail and ran downstairs, freaking, oh, I do not like this, oh, I do not like this, and flushed it down the toilet.

Each day I would pray to the Lord, "Father, when my settlement comes in, all I want is a little house in the country that is warm for us all and a garden for my dogs to play in, with your beautiful trees around."

Mark 11:24-25 Therefore I say unto you, what things soever ye desire when ye pray, believe that ye receive them, and ye shall have them. And when ye stand praying, forgive, if ye have ought against any: that your Father which is in heaven may forgive you your trespasses.

One day, walking the dogs across the fields, we were at the far end of the field, away from home, when I saw a Coyote. I knew they were around, as I could hear them, especially if they had caught an animal; the noise was horrendous. I remember back on the estate; I would listen to them; it was a chilling sound that one never forgets. Now, this day, as I saw this coyote coming out of the mist, I thought to myself, where there is one, there will be more. I prayed, "Dear Lord, please get us home safely." I started to see another coyote; knowing not to run, I whispered to the dogs, "Come, let us get back home." The dogs had sensed the presence of the Coyotes, and their shackles were raised. I know the Lord had an angel on guard for us to get us safely home.

During this time at the cottage, my friend Ellen invited me to supper and go afterward to the candlelight parade held every Christmas. They had invited a friend of Ellen's husband, John, to dinner. Mike was in the army, based in Winnipeg, where John used to be before his retirement. The evening was lovely, and we all had an enjoyable time singing carols and drinking hot mulled cider and mince pies. Mike invited me out for a meal the following week. He seemed nice and was a gentleman towards me. However, I made it clear that there would not be a relationship, just a friendship.

We would meet for a game of cards or go for a walk with the dogs. Nevertheless, over two to three months, Mike started talking about taking me on holiday; as he spoke about the holiday and about staying in a motel, I said, "We would have to have separate rooms," Mike said, "What? For?" "I'm not paying for two rooms when we can share a room." I said, "There is no way that I will be sharing a room with you." He became persistent; however, I refused the idea. Then whenever Mike saw me after this, he started pushing himself towards me, trying to put his arms around me. I did not want this, and I told him so directly. When he had left, I prayed to the Lord, "Father, something is not right about the friendship that I have with Mike, something is very wrong, please help and guide me, show me what I need to know, please, dear Father?" I pleaded. I saw a black spot about Mike; therefore, I knew the Lord was warning me away from him. I decided to call Mike and end the friendship. My friends Ellen and John were unhappy with me, saying that I had hurt their friend. Nevertheless, as far as I was concerned, the friendship was ended.

CHAPTER 10

A NEW JOB AND A NEW HOME

On my walks with my dogs, I had met a lady around my age who had a lovely German Shepherd. I quite liked her; however, she was not a Christian and our views did differ on different things, but I accepted her for who she was, and we became good friends. We met up quite regularly in our walks, met at each other's homes, and went shopping together.

While working for the Surgeon, I received a call from Ellen, saying that there was a job opening in the administration department of a large retail chain store in the centre of Winnipeg, and would I be interested in it? If I were, she would arrange an appointment for me to go in for an interview. I was shocked and said, "Yes, I would be very interested in the job." The date for the interview was given, and I arranged to have time off from work to be able to go. I was nervous, as I was to sit a test. I had not fully completed the test when the supervisor came in to say the time was up. I apologized, saying that I had not completed the test. The lady said that very few applicants finished the test, not to worry. I will run the test results and see how you managed. A brief time later, she returned all smiles, saying that I had passed. The supervisor then informed me about the job and what my work would involve; it was exciting.

Especially when she informed me of the benefits of the job, plus the wage, I thought, thank You, Lord. We arranged that I would start my new career in two weeks to be able to give the Surgeon time to find a replacement for me. The drive was forty-five minutes, there and back, plus finding a place to park. I ended up parking my car out of the town centre on one of the side streets. Therefore, I had to allow myself more time in the morning to get to work on time. The job took a little while to get used to; however, I managed and enjoyed the work. Yes, it was tiring and stressful, but I was determined to succeed at it. During my time in the administration office, my lawyer was sent an appointment for me to see a particular doctor, who I would have to travel two hours to see. Therefore, I would need time off to go to the appointment. Paul had planned to take me as he knew driving any distance was still extremely hard for me. My lawyer had told me that this was an essential appointment about my accident. I went and spoke to my supervisor about the meeting and how necessary it was for me to go. However, she would not allow me to have time off to go. I went back to my desk, devastated, and could not stop the tears from pouring down my face. I prayed, "Dear Jesus, what am I going to do?" One of the other supervisors came in to speak to my supervisor, saw what a state I was in, and inquired what was going on? By this other supervisor intervening, who, I might add, had superiority over my supervisor, I would be allowed to go because of the intervention. I could not thank Jesus enough. I should add that I kept a small Precious Moments Bible on my desk and had it opened to:

Lamentations 3:21-26 This I recall to my mind, therefore have, I hope. 22. It is of the Lord's mercies that we are not consumed because His compassions fail not. 23. They are new every morning: great is thy faithfulness. 24. The Lord is my portion, saith my soul, therefore will I hope in Him. 25. The Lord is good unto them that wait for Him, to the soul that seeketh Him. 26. It is good that a man should both hope and quietly wait for the salvation of the Lord. Amen

It was now four years since my accident, and my lawyer phoned to say, "I expect your settlement cheque to come in very soon, start looking for your new home." I did this with the help of an agent, who took me to see a particular home in the country. It was lovely; however, the price was more than I could afford. Two months later, the same agent phoned me again to say that a previous buyer's offer on the house that I had seen had fallen through, and the house was back up for sale at a much lower price, one that I should be able to afford. Once again, we made the appointment to view the house. As we drove close to the home, I could see that it looked like a little cottage amongst beautiful Pine trees. The home's inside was lovely and warm, with two bedrooms, a living room, a beautiful eat-in kitchen, and an on-suite bathroom that could also be accessed from the living room. Then down a couple of stairs to the stone-paved sunroom, looking out onto a lovely garden with fruit trees and the most beautiful weeping birches I had ever seen. As I was leaving to get into the car, the Lord stopped me and said, "Take a look around you." Lord, you have answered my prayer. It was the little house in the country, with a garden for my dogs. "Oh Lord, this is what I had prayed for; look at those beautiful trees."

Excited, I said to the agent, "I will make an offer." After going back and forth a couple of times, we all agreed on the price. I was overjoyed and could not stop praising the Lord. "Father, how faithful you are to me." The next day, I phoned my bank manager. To arrange with my lawyer for the settlement to go down on the house. I then asked him if I would be able to have a small mortgage of about $4,000.00 to cover sundries, such as fencing, gates for my dogs, and paying the Solicitor's bills to purchase the house. The manager brought my request to the board, knowing I was in bankruptcy still and that I would have my answer by Thursday. Every moment I could, I prayed the promises of God from my little Bible, the bank gave me my mortgage. God is so faithful and to be praised.

My friends from church arranged to move my furniture into my new home; I was so excited and felt so blessed by the Lord. Amy, my friend with the German Shepherd, said that she would pick up fish and chips for us to eat. We picnicked on the living room floor. Then together, we went back to the house, packed up my belongings in boxes, and moved them into our cars to take over to the home. Tomorrow, the men would be moving all the furniture into the new house. It was February and very cold; oh, the warmth of the new home was so incredible. Thank you, Jesus; I cannot thank you enough for what You have done for me. I prayed silently.

After a while at my church, the pastor wanted us to pray in tongues. I did start doing this for a time, and then I started thinking to myself, do I know what I am saying when I do this? The answer was no. Then I started paying more attention to what was going on and how the pastor tried to force people to pray in tongues. I thought to myself, this is so wrong; if the Lord gave us the gift of speaking in tongues, this would come naturally, not forced. I became increasingly uncomfortable with what was going on. Then one day, it all came to a head. I prayed, dear Father, I cannot go on with this; please show me what to do? I knew a Baptist church was at the end of my road, so I started attending. The teaching was much better than at my earlier church, plus no speaking in tongues. I started learning so much more, and the whole atmosphere was different. Then one day, the pastor spoke on the humility of foot washing that Jesus did for His disciples and that he would like to start it in the church and asked if anyone wanted to be involved, pick a partner, and come down the front. I could tell the Holy Spirit was wanting me to do this. I turned; there was a woman my age; I walked over to her and held out my hand; she walked with me to where a bowl of water and a towel had been put for foot washing.

What a humbling experience, the woman's name was Ruth, and that became the start of a beautiful friendship between me and her, plus her family. I do not remember the church ever doing that again. After this, I asked the pastor if I could be involved in the choir? The pastor introduced me to the choir director, who suggested that I would be a second soprano and where I should sit in the choir. Being part of this choir was terrific, and I enjoyed this. The practice sessions we had each week were fun; the choir director made the sessions so enjoyable, and the songs he and his wife chose were so beautiful, harmonizing, like the angels singing. I was thrilled here at this church, and I felt settled.

I had a two-week holiday coming, so I prayed about where I could go and take the dogs with me. I found pamphlets on Nova Scotia. The place looked lovely; however, could I drive that far? I phoned the CAA that I belonged to and asked them if they could send me directions, a time scale, and places to stay on the trip. They did; later that week, I received the information from them. The trip would be at least 2300 miles and take at least 33 Hrs. So, I would travel down through Ontario, part of Quebec, New Brunswick, and Nova Scotia. They had outlined the motels for me to stay in with the dogs. I phoned a B & B in Nova Scotia who could put me up with the dogs, saying that she had a large trailer hooked up where I could sleep with the dogs and come into the house for my meals, which sounded terrific. I had been praying about this and felt that the Lord would be helping me on my travels. Nevertheless, this was something huge for me to do, however, I knew that the Lord would be with me every part of the journey, was I scared, yes, a little but my hope and courage was in the Lord. Therefore, I arranged bookings with motels for traveling to Nova Scotia, then back again when it was time for me to return.

The drive was incredible; the beauty that I was seeing all of God's beautiful creations. As I left Winnipeg, Ontario, the air in New Brunswick had changed; it was clear, pure fresh air up in the hills of New Brunswick, then down into Nova Scotia, how magnificent everything looked. It was lovely at the B & B, high on a hill above the sea. During my time there, walking on the sands at the beach, I was praying, "Lord, when it is time for me to retire, would you bring me back here, please?" I loved Nova Scotia so much. The dogs had the time of their lives, dashing into the sea. The first time they ran into the sea, the look on their faces as they tasted seawater did not deter them; they were having a wonderful time. The holiday did me a lot of good, fresh sea air, warmth, and relaxation; it was truly remarkable. It was a holiday to be remembered. The time went by too fast, and it was time to say goodbye and return on our journey home. The Lord had his loving arm around us as we journeyed back home in safety.

Philippians 4:6-7 Be careful for nothing, but in everything by prayer and supplication with thanksgiving let your requests be made known unto God. 7. And the peace of God, which passeth all understanding, shall keep your hearts and minds through Christ Jesus.

At home, I had already had the fence and gates put up for the dogs to have a large area for running and playing in. We had lovely walks to go on in the morning and evening. I loved it where we lived. Off the one side of the garden was a large nursery that the earlier owner had put up, so I decided to use it for chickens to have my eggs. I bought twelve young chicks, and when it was time, I put them in the nursery where they could scratch around. Then I thought it would be nice if they could get out into the garden, so I built a ladder for them to go from the window into the garden how; they loved this. Sandy and Mickey loved their extended family as they walked them around the garden. When I would come home from work at night, the dogs and chickens would run to the fence to greet me. I called the chickens my girls. They loved to be picked up and nestle under my chin, and they were so warm and soft. I started to collect eggs from them and would sell the eggs that I did not need. Ruth and her family had eggs from me, and because Ruth and her husband had a beehive, I would buy honey from her; it was delicious. We helped each other out.

Ruth and I would ride our bikes around the area, and one day, she said to me, "Do you want to try rollerblading?" I agreed to try, so we rode our bikes down to an area where we could do that. We put our blades on, then started. We were coming to a wooden bridge, so I thought, if I hopped over the edge of the bridge, I would be fine!! Guess what? I crashed into the bridge railings; I was not OK, which put an end to that for the day.

Back at work, it was becoming a different story; I was under a lot of stress; even though I enjoyed the work that I was doing and knew that I was doing an excellent job, work hours were changing, we were required to work from nine in the morning to sometimes nine to ten at night. The stress and late nights were becoming too much for me, and eventually, I became ill. Leaving work one night, I decided to drive to a clinic where I lived and saw a doctor there. Upon examining me, he said, "You are ill; no work for you for two weeks." I phoned my supervisor about what the doctor said, and she told me, "You will report for work tomorrow; I said to her, "I cannot; I have been taken ill." "You will come into work." She hung up on me. The next day, my supervisor phoned me and said, "I was to come straight into work." Of course, I was not able to. Every day, she would phone me; I was flooded with tears on the floor and became even sicker. I went to see my doctor again, who put me in the care of a consultant, who told me that I would have to stop working, my nervous system and my body were breaking down, and I would get worse if I did not listen his advice. Therefore, with the consultant's help, I was able to go on disability. The consultant wrote to my work with a report of my illness. Then I received a letter from my supervisor, who accused me of job abandonment. This letter I sent to my lawyer telling him what had happened. I called Human Resources at the head office of the store chain where I worked. I did this, and they took care of the problem for me.

Then one day, after a dizzy spell, I laid down and cried out to the Lord, "Father, what do you want me to do?" The still small voice of the Holy Spirit came to me, "I want you to sell this home." "Oh, Lord," I cried out to Him, "This beautiful home that You gave to me, and, I know, You can take it away again...please, Father, give me confirmation in the morning, fill me with your song and Your Word, so I know this is from you, please?"

The following day, as I woke up, I felt different; there was no foreboding about leaving this home, where I had been for the last two years; I had a sense that the Lord was leading me in a different direction that He was in charge. I could not stop praising the Lord, He filled me with excellent confirmation from His Word, and I could not stop singing songs of praises, glorifying my God.

Jeremiah 29:11-14 For I know the thoughts that I think toward you, saith the Lord, thoughts of peace, and not of evil, to give you an expected end. Then shall ye call upon me, and I will hearken unto you. And ye shall seek me and find me when ye shall search for me with all your heart. And I will be found of you, saith the Lord.

I phoned a Christian estate agent I knew from my church and told him that the Lord asked me to sell my home. He said he would pray about it and get back to me.

CHAPTER 11

NOVA SCOTIA

As the weeks and months went by, I was still very unwell; however, I had been journaling what the Lord was telling me in the scriptures that He was giving me as I spent each day with Him in His Word. One day, I asked the Lord, "Father, where are you sending me?" I will need a new home. Suddenly, the still, small voice of the Holy Spirit said, "I am sending you to Nova Scotia." I suddenly realized what the Lord was doing for me. I had been heartbroken so many times over my sons.

I remembered their weddings and how they had broken my heart. How my younger son had led me to believe he wanted photos of when he was a baby for himself, and I willingly had given him photo's that I had. I sat at his wedding reception with my uncle, cousin, and mum. Seeing the picture's that I had given him portrayed on a screen as a baby, with his dad. They had not included me, and it was as if I had not been there when he was a baby. Why did he deceive me, not telling me the truth? When I had spent so much time making all the gifts for the guests. I drove up to my daughter-in-law to do her makeup on their wedding day; I loved her as my daughter; how could she have deceived me. It was as if I had never existed. I was so glad my uncle was there; he could see how hurt I was; he was the one who comforted me. I wish I had never gone to that wedding. At my elder son's wedding, he had refused to let Paul bring me to the wedding, so I had to rely on my younger son and his wife to take me.

At the reception, I was to regret ever having gone there. Unfortunately, the table we were to sit at was upfront, with my younger son and his wife in front of everyone. However, they did not stay with me; wanting to visit their friends and family. Finding myself alone in front of these strangers, I wanted to disappear, but I had nowhere to go. When the dancing started, not once did my elder son ask me to dance with him; he ignored me the whole time. I could not stop tears coming into my eyes, but I refused to let them flow. Again, I wished I had never gone to the wedding. I could not leave as my younger son, and his wife had brought me. How could my sons do this to me? These weddings had put me through too much stress. Dear Lord, I prayed, please help me?

Knowing that my elder son would come down to visit relatives that lived around the corner from me yet would not see me hurt me very much. If I visited my younger son and his wife, Brian would be there with his wife on occasions, and it was more than I could manage.

The Lord was taking me away from all the grief. Or was He taking me on a journey to weaken or strengthen my faith with my Father in heaven? Little did I know what horrors were awaiting me ahead.

Now, back to Nova Scotia, where I had been once before for a beautiful holiday with Sandy and Mickey. Now to get out the map of Nova Scotia, as I looked at the map, I was looking at where I had been before on the south shore and remembering the prayer that I had uttered to the Lord walking along the beautiful sandy beach with my dogs. "Oh Lord, I pray that you will bring me back here when I am retired; it is so beautiful and peaceful here." Little did I know at that time, the

Lord was going to answer my prayer far sooner than I had expected. Now looking at the map of Nova Scotia, I prayed, "Father, where are you going to send me?" The Lord lifted my eyes to the northern part; suddenly, I burst out, "What is up there, Lord?" My eyes were resting on the Northumberland Strait, way at the tip of Nova Scotia.

The Lord showed me to leave my past and my family behind and start something new in my life. "Oh Father," I prayed; I will follow You wherever You want me to go. God would be taking me away from all the grief I had experienced; my son's, whom I loved, who had broken my heart. My mother thought she should get my settlement. All the horror God was going to put behind me.

My real estate agent had gotten back to me and would be listing my house for sale. I asked him if he could get me in touch with an agent in Nova Scotia for me to view homes. He did this for me, and the following day I received a call from the agent in Nova Scotia, and we agreed that I would fly out there to meet her and view the homes she would have for me to see. The night before I met the agent, I prayed, "Lord, You, show me the house that You want me to have, and make it loud and clear for me so that I know for sure. Be my constant guide as I want to be where You want me to be, not where I want to be, for You alone, know what is best for me, thank you, Father, Amen."

The year was October 1995. Flying out to meet with the agent, who said upon my arrival, "I have six homes to show you." So, off we went. The Lord was not in any of the houses. However, as we started up a particular country road, I suddenly said to the agent, "That's the house over there," she looked at me strangely, and as we went up the driveway, I knew this was the house. We went to the back door and climbed up the stairs; opening the door into the kitchen, the Lord was letting me know, loud and clear, and before I saw the rest of the house, I said, "I am putting in an offer." The Lord gave me more extensive and even better than I could imagine, so many trees and woods on twenty-two acres of property. The people accepted my offer, and I went back to the airport to fly to Winnipeg. There had been no offers on my home, and by April 1996, the six-month contract that I had on the house in Nova Scotia was up. However, I knew that if the Lord wanted me there in that home, I would be there. I had the strongest feeling that I would be in Nova Scotia by the end of August 1996.

Shortly after this, there were friends that I would meet with, and we would discuss Bible passages and help each other out. At her home, I heard a dog barking during this time, so I said to her, "You have a dog?" "Yes," she said; we do not know what to do with him; we keep him tied up in the basement. I said, "You what," "Let me see the dog?" I went down the basement stairs, and there was this little Cocker Spaniel tied up down there. I said to my friend, "Please, let him loose?" She did this; I just sat on the stairs and talked to the dog, coaxing him towards me, then he was in my arms. I just spoke gently to the little dog, and he nestled in with me. My friend said they would take it to the Humane Society as they did not want the dog. I said, "Please let me take the dog home with me; I will look after him. I did this; now Sandy and Mickey had a new companion. One big happy family, the three dogs and the chickens got along.

During this time, I phoned Ellen, my friend, who I had not seen since I stopped seeing Mike and asked her if she wanted to come around for a visit and a cup of tea. She agreed. While talking with Ellen, she mentioned that Mike was depressed and desperately needed friends and that he had been back in Winnipeg for a while now. As Ellen spoke to me about his situation, I felt compassion for him welling up in me. So, I said to Ellen, "Do you think he would like me to write to him? however, I do not know his address." Ellen said, "I think he would appreciate hearing from you." I will get the address for you. She did this. A week after I had written to Mike, I received a phone call from him, saying how pleased and surprised he was to hear from me. We talked for a while, and "I said we should keep in touch." We did most days, talking to each other. Mike knew I was not well and was not getting any better. Due to my physical and mental incapacity, I was having difficulty getting organized. I preferred to spend time with the Lord, journaling to read His scriptures and walking my dogs.

In June that year, Mike said he wanted to marry me and take care of me. I did not want to get married again; however, I did need someone to take care of me. Even though we both lived in Manitoba, Mike was living in Winnipeg, this was still quite a distance from where I lived in Minnedosa, so Mike arranged to come down to see me. The day he arrived, he was so pleased to see me, and that evening, he took me to a Chinese restaurant, proposed to me, and gave me a beautiful engagement ring. The evening was lovely. We discussed when we should be married and to plan the wedding. No offers had come in on my home; however, I had such a firm conviction that the Lord would be moving things along for me. Therefore, I believed that we would be in Nova Scotia by the end of August that year. I believed by faith that this would happen. Mike, however, did not have this conviction; nevertheless, I was sure.

Isaiah 40: 31 But they that wait upon the Lord shall renew their strength; they shall mount up with wings as eagles; they shall run, and not be weary, and they shall walk and not faint.

Was there love between Mike and me? No, the relationship was more of companionship?

In the second week of August that year, I had an offer on my home. It was deficient, so I took it to the Lord and asked, "Father, what do You want me to do about this offer?" The still small voice of the Holy Spirit said." Give unto others who have less than you." Therefore, I accepted the offer. I then contacted the agent in Nova Scotia and asked if the house was still available? It was, so I went in with a lower offer. The people accepted the offer. Mike and I decided to rent a U-Haul to transport all my furnishings and belongings. We then arranged for someone to drive the truck out there, and Mike and I would follow in our cars, me with my dogs. We decided to get married in September that year, and I asked my friend Ruth if she would be my Bridesmaid and Amy if she would be my Maid of Honour? They agreed and would fly out to Nova Scotia before the wedding, stay a couple of days, then fly back again. Mike and I found a B & B for our wedding night. Little did I know that my nightmare was about to begin.

Psalm 146: 3 Put not your trust in princes, nor in the son of man, in whom there is no help.

The good Lord never promised to heal me; I still suffer from the injuries compounded by other injuries incurred in the next part of my life story. I now know my limitations and am not worried, as I know who oversees my life, My Lord and Saviour Jesus Christ.

Jesus has seen me through every step and has promised never to leave me or forsake me in His Word. He is always with me and will continue to be with me through the horrors of my life. I am and have been on a journey with my Lord. I have been on a fulfilling journey with my Saviour and my Forever Friend. Who has been with me on the mountain tops and in the dark valleys?

He will hold me fast, for my Saviour loves me so.

CHAPTER 12

FAITH IS TESTED

When I arrived in Nova Scotia, little did I realize that from 1996, when I came, till 2005, my faith in the Lord was going to be seriously tested? I had no idea that I would be traveling through the valley of the shadow of death with my Shepherd.

I was so excited as we reached the new home. My furniture fitted into the rooms perfectly; the only obstacle was my piano, Mike had tied a rope to the leg of it, and it had snapped in the journey, I was not pleased about that as the piano was an old Nord Heimer piano with a beautiful sound to it. I would have to find someone who could mend it. Since coming to Nova Scotia, Mike's mood was fluctuating, and I was not sure why, so I let him be. The week before the wedding, I went down to the airport to meet my friends and bring them back home. It was lovely seeing them again. The day of the wedding arrived, I wore a two-piece soft flowing suit, it was beautiful. I did not want another wedding dress. My bridesmaids were ready, and we travelled down to the church. The wedding was formal, with my girlfriends and Mike's two friends, a husband and a wife that lived in Nova Scotia. The pastor was a lovely man, and I felt comfortable with him. After the wedding, Mike's friends had arranged for us to go back to their place for the reception, as they lived near the church. We all enjoyed ourselves, and then it was time to go home. Mike and I had booked into a B & B and would be having supper there, then breakfast in the morning, before we came back to the house. The girls would be staying at home. When we arrived back at the house later that morning, my friends and the dogs were there to greet us. When it was time for bed that night, Mike played cards with Amy, and Ruth and I went up to our different beds. I could see Ruth's face at the fact that Mike was staying downstairs to play cards with Amy; this was reminiscent of my first marriage, I did not know what to think.

I loved my new home and the surrounding area; it was peaceful. I met my neighbors, who were lovely people, and had them in for tea. Their son had looked after the house and grounds when the woman who had owned the home had died. I would often visit with my neighbor for a cup of tea. She was Norwegian, and I liked her. They were to prove to be good neighbors.

Mike liked to work outside, which was fine. I would walk the dogs on the trails and could be gone walking for two hours. I was so happy walking the trails with the dogs. It was out in nature, clambering over rocks and small gulley's, seeing where we could go. There was a large pond on the property, and there was an otter in the pond. Sandy thought this was wonderful, she would jump in the water and try and swim up to the Otter, but before she had gotten near it, the Otter would slam his tail in the water and race back to the other end. Poor Sandy, as hard as she tried, was not fast enough. Mickey would stand there barking at her to come back. Mike and I found a Baptist church that we would attend, there were lovely friendly people there, and we liked the pastor. One day we invited the pastor and his wife back for dinner. He said to us, "All the time I have been at this church, you are the first people to invite us back."

I was shocked by this; anyway, they came back to the house, and we had a lovely time with them.

Mike and I decided to put in a wood stove to help heat the house; we found a store, found the stove that we liked, and chose stone tile to go on the floor around the stove. The men came in to fit the stove and the chimney, which would make the room even cosier. I found out from my neighbors that I could join the forest co-op in town. I did and ordered a truckload of logs. Now, it was to get them all cut up ready to use. There was a garage, and we could store the wood there.

Unfortunately, I did not know the man I had married; it had not been a love marriage but for convenience. As the weeks and months went by, it was like being on a roller coaster. The coercive control was like a recap of my marriage to Brian, having to be compliant and willing to please. The physical and mental stress became much worse. Mike was perverse in how he treated me, not as a husband should treat his wife; his sexual abuse and rape were continuous. I would be asleep when I would suddenly feel hands around my neck in a stranglehold, then raping me, pulling my hair back tight, and raping me again. I could not move, for fear had engulfed me. I would never see his face as he always came from behind me. Our marriage was a sham. I ended up having panic attacks every time he came near me. Things had deteriorated so much. How was I going to cope with this? "O Father, I need your help and advice?"

1Peter 1:7 and 13 That the trial of your faith, being much more precious than of gold that perishes, though it is tried with fire, might be found unto praise and honour and glory at the appearing of Jesus Christ. 13. Wherefore gird up the loins of your mind, be sober, and hope to the end for the grace that is to be brought unto you at the revelation of Jesus Christ.

Nights would find me downstairs, hugging my Bible, and Sandy, my Retriever, crying out to the Lord, "What have I done? O Father, forgive me, a sinner, for getting myself into this situation. I had forgotten what the Lord had shown me about Mike when I met him. Now, I realized why the Lord had warned me. Little did I know that Mike was stalking me. I would escape to the trails with the dogs, singing to the Lord at the top of my voice, trying to still the fear in me. When returning home, Mike said to me, "You know, I can see you, but you will not be able to see me. Wherever you go, I will be watching you." Not only did he do this, but whenever I wanted to make a phone call, he would be on the receiver in the next room listening. His coercive control was debilitating, and I felt like I was in prison.

When I went to get groceries, Mike always had to come and follow me around the store wearing his heavy boots, stomping them on the floor with every step. So much fear was building up in me. However, regarding my dogs, if I heard them cry out, I would come running down the stairs to see what was happening and looked to see Mikey, quivering and shaking in fear, picking him up and holding him tightly to me, I would be on Mike like a ton of bricks, saying, "What have you done to him?" All fear would be gone; I did not care about myself; however, I warned him if I ever caught him hurting my dogs, he would be out of the house for good.

We had been married for almost ten months if you can call it that. Mike had gone down to Halifax to see his friends for the weekend and was coming back on Monday. I spent this time with the Lord, crying out to Him, "Father, what can I do?" Then a still small voice of the Holy Spirit said to me, "Look in the bottom drawer of Mike's filing cabinet." I said, "O Lord, I'm afraid to look; the still small voice of the Holy Spirit beckoned to me again, "Go and Look; you will see what you need to know." I went and gingerly looked, there were files, and as I went through them, I came to this file. "O dear Father, O no." I felt sick, dirty that Mike had ever touched me, and the acute realization of whom I had married. Mike was a Paedophile who had been to prison for the sexual molestation of young girls and his daughter. The horror was magnifying in me. I wrapped my arms around myself and howled in agony. How do I get out of this? Suddenly realizing that the phone was ringing, I answered it. It was my neighbor; she said, "Whatever is the matter? I will be right over." The neighborhood knew about Mike; he had been in the papers when he was arrested by the RCMP upon his arrival back to his barracks in Winnipeg from tour duty. All my neighbors thought I had known about Mike, which I had not. Now everything started to make sense.

Since arriving in Nova Scotia, I had started a care group in my home; I would phone neighbors and invite them to the group. To know each other, helping where we can; however, the actual evening would be to study the Bible, sing hymns and worship songs, and get everyone involved. This Monday, my neighbor, Angela, had me and the dogs come back to her home with her. Meanwhile, she contacted everyone in our care group to ask them to meet at her house instead and explain what had happened. When Mike returned from Halifax and found that I was not at home, neither were the dogs. He phoned Angela's house and asked if I was there. Telling him that I was there, then told her to ask me to come home at once. When I did not return home, Mike drove to Angela's house in a mad rush, showering stones as he came to a halt in his car in her driveway. He stormed out of the vehicle and demanded that I get in the car. I refused; instead, I told him to pack his bags, get out of the house, and not return. He was so angry; his acerbity was awful. I started to recoil; however, the care group was there, and they surrounded me and told him to go and pack his bags and that he had thirty minutes to get out; if he was not out by then, they were going to call the police.

Angela's husband, Bob, who worked at a hardware store, said that he would change all the locks in the house in case Mike came back that night. Then a couple of days later, I started receiving threatening phone calls from Mike, so I called the police, who also were aware of him. They created a report on Mike. Then Mike phoned to say that it did not matter about changing the locks, as he knew every square inch of the house and that he could get in if he wanted to. He kept phoning me, and then I started to receive malicious letters from Mike, stating that he had informed my friends and relatives on our computer that he had taken, which held all their addresses and phone numbers. The awful things he said that he had told people about me, one letter from my brother's wife, who said how sick I must be. These horrendous letters took a massive toll on me, and I was so stressed out.

The police started to watch me and my property because of all the threats I received from Mike. My doctor was relieved that Mike had gone. When we lived together, I was always ending up in the hospital with severe panic attacks; the doctor said he would send me to Dartmouth to see a psychiatrist who deals with high anxiety and panic attacks. The psychiatrist was such a kind man and helped me so much. This time on a visit to him, the psychiatrist would go into my past with Brian. As we talked about what had happened in the marriage, I became upset that the marriage to Brian and the circumstances that I found myself in had changed me; I was not the same person that I once was, and just howled out, "O my sons, my sons," how I longed to hold them in my arms again. The psychiatrist moved his chair beside me, held my hand, and talked gently to me until I stopped crying. I wished that I could block out that terrible time. My sons, to this day, have never known what I went through with their father. They had once told me that Brian had called them together and gave his version of what went on in that marriage; however, I could not say anything; I never wanted to talk about it; it was too traumatizing.

One day, on my visit to the psychiatrist, I asked if he would mind reading the letters I had received from Mike. I needed reassurance that I was not reading into them something that was not there. I was in such a state of mind. The psychiatrist started to read them, then looked at me and said, "This man is evil; you must have a Peace Bond against him. He then wrote a letter for me to take to the court in Truro. I had by now found out that Mike had a probation officer. So, I informed the psychiatrist of this fact. He said to let the probation officer see these letters and then for the officer to give them to the prosecutor and one to be given to the judge on the court day. I did and was given a court date. I had friends go with me on the court date, as my psychiatrist warned me not to travel to Truro alone, where Mike was living. My psychiatrist was worried about my safety. The judge awarded me the Peace Bond, then asked me how long I wanted it? I said, "Can I have it forever?" No, dear, but I will grant you the maximum of a year. The year was 1997. One year later, we were divorced. Nevertheless, this was not going to stop him from causing trouble for me. Mike would continue to stalk me until I left Canada in 2014.

Psalm 31:7 and 24. I will be glad and rejoice in thy mercy: for thou hast considered my trouble; thou hast known my soul in adversities. 24. Be of good courage, and He shall strengthen your heart, all ye that hope in the Lord.

CHAPTER 13

MORE TESTING

Determination and hope in the Lord started me off on a new life. I began to attend the Presbyterian church in the village where I lived and became involved in Bible study. There was going to be a change in my life now. A better life for my precious dogs, who helped me through the trials and tribulations I had been going through. To curl up with these special dogs and cuddle them was so wonderful, without the fear of Mike coming in. Even though I still walked the trails with the dogs, I could not help but look over my shoulder to see if anyone was watching me.

1Peter 5:6-7 Humble yourselves therefore under the mighty hand of God that He may exalt you in due time. 7. Casting all your care upon Him, for He careth for you.

Needing to give the house a fresh look and wipe away all horror of what had taken place inside, I needed to investigate renovations on the house; Even though I still lived in fear of Mike, I refused to allow my fears to take me captive. I knew without a doubt that Jesus was with me and knew that He would never leave me or forsake me. I had found a DIY man that worked down the road in a wood mill and asked him when he had the time if he would come and give me a quote on new windows, a new framework for inside the living room. I wanted to take the wall down that separated the living room from the sunroom and make it one large room with a cathedral ceiling in the sunroom area. I bought beautiful wallpaper that would make the room cosy yet bright. To help the DIY man, I started taking the dividing wall apart, and it was amazing all the old newspapers that I found inside the wall were used for insulating the wall. The DIY man told me to go to the hardware store and ask to see the windows that they had in storage. I found the ones I wanted for the house and bought them, so the DIY man could pick them up when he was ready to install them. The DIY man had done an excellent job on the finished cathedral ceiling, giving the room an airy look. The DIY man installed the new windows and built a wide windowsill in front of the windows, which was effective in the room, and I completed the wallpapering. The room looked lovely; I was so pleased with the work done. The home now had a fresh look. Later I was informed that I could have had a grant from the government for the job done. No one had told me of that, and I was not aware of grants for homes.

I had a woman friend that I had met at physiotherapy, she had seemed lonely, so I befriended her. During the weeks that I saw Jean, one of her dogs had died, and she was very distressed. After a couple of weeks, she said she would like to get another dog. I had seen an advert in the paper for husky pups free to a loving home. I told Jean about this, and she said that she would like to go and look. So, I planned with the breeder for us to go there. On arriving there, the place was huge, and we learned that they export their dogs worldwide. The breeder took us to where there were pups lined up; oh, these precious creatures, I thought to myself. Jean chose a lovely pure white Siberian Husky. Jean planned with the vet to have the pup spaded. The day Jean was to pick the puppy up and bring her home, unknown to me, Jean put the puppy in an outside pen, then went off to meet her friends. Jean phoned me to see if I would go over to watch the dog. The day was raining hard; I thought to myself, the pup should not be outside in this when it had been operated on that day. So, I drove my car over to Jean's home; on arriving, I was horrified to see that the pup had clawed its way out of the pen and was leaning against the house wall, shivering. I picked the poor little thing up and took her into Jean's house, down to her basement, grabbed a towel, poured warm water into the sink, and gently put the pup in the warm water to warm her up and clean the mud off her. Then wrapped her up in a towel to dry her, then wrapped her in another towel to take her home with me. I was so angry with Jean that she had thought only of herself and not the pup. At home, I laid the puppy down in a warm blanket. However, that night the puppy started to have loose bloody diarrhea. I realized that the pup was ill. So, I phoned the vet and explained what had happened. However, she told me what to do if the puppy was no better to bring her down to the surgery first thing in the morning. I phoned Jean that night and told her what had happened and that we had to get the pup to the vet first thing in the morning. She was not too happy but agreed. The puppy had to be put on a drip as she was ill. When the vet phoned me that the pup could go home, I let Jean know, as she would have to pay the vet costs. Driving back home with the puppy, I said to Jean, take me to my place, please? We went indoors at my home, and I laid the pup on a blanket so that she could have a sleep. I said to Jean, "I cannot believe what you did to that poor animal; how could you do such a thing? Jean, I am not letting you take this pup home; she will stay here with me." I was not at all happy with her. Our relationship was never the same after that. I called the pup Anika, and she was the first Siberian Husky that I rescued; she turned into a beautiful dog. I had Sandy, Mickey, Mikey the Spaniel, and Anika. Shortly after this, I rescued another Siberian Husky, Tovia. The year was 1998, the year I started my Siberian Husky Rescue. These beautiful dogs would come to have such a meaning to me and would always have a place in my life, even to this day that I am writing my memoir.

When I was a teenager, I used to love ice skating. I would go to the Dublin arena in Ireland, where I grew up, put my skates on and go out onto the ice and lose myself in the music as I skated around to my heart's content. Thinking about this, I went off and bought myself a pair of skates in the second-hand store in the village. Then off I went to the arena, had the skates sharpened in case they were blunt. Putting the skates on, I went slowly onto the ice. Getting into the movement with the music, I thought, how lovely it is to be skating again and to feel free as a bird. Then, Bang, what was that noise? Why does my head hurt so badly? I had fallen back on my head and was lying there semi-conscious. I could hear voices around me but could not focus on anything or anyone; everything was a blur. Next, paramedics lifted me onto an ambulance, then the pain; I was still in and out of consciousness; my doctor was speaking to me, but I could not say anything, plus he was in and out of my vision. Then an agonizing trip down to Halifax. Another severe head injury. After a time, I recovered from this head injury too. However, no more skating for me.

I focused all my attention on my dogs, these blessed gifts from God. We would have fun up the trails. I would let them run loose; however, Anika and Tovia had on a double harness that would keep them together. One day, going by the pond, did not the little monkeys run in the pond and up to the Beaver dam that the Beavers had built. There entwined around the branches of the dam, looking at me as if to say, look at us, mum. So, I had to take off my sneakers and walk into the pond that was all slimy and not very nice over to where they were. They thought it was fun; meanwhile, the other dogs watched. I managed to free them and get back to the path with them. This time they were put on a leash so that I could have control of them.

Another time, we were going up the trails further to where there was another pond, it was iced over, and Micky spotted a Mongoose at the end of the pond, so he decided he would go after the Mongoose. Mickey, meanwhile, had also spotted the Mongoose, and he was barking at Micky to come back, as the Mongoose can be dangerous. Mickey looked quite funny as he barked; he was lifting himself off the ground and trying to warn Micky to come back. Nothing the dogs or I could do would get Micky's attention away from the Mongoose, so I said to Micky, "Bye, Micky, we are going back home." We went a little way; then I called out, "Micky come on." It was not until we were home that Micky came running back, his ears flying as he tore into the garden. I said to him, "Did you have fun?" He was a happy little fellow.

During this time, I had started my care group up again. We had such a lovely time discussing Bible verses and singing. We always had a fellowship supper afterward; there was such a friendly group of people there, usually about twenty. I had friends who had become missionaries and needed a car. So, I took this to the Lord in prayer and asked the Lord if I should give them my car? I did, knowing that the Lord would provide for me. The year was now two thousand, and I needed a car; nevertheless, did I go before the Lord? The next thing I did, I think the excitement of ordering a new Windstar van from the Ford Dealership went to my head.

Psalm 37:34 Wait on the Lord and keep His way. I forgot to wait on the Lord for a car, I went ahead of Him, and it was my downfall. Why did I order the van? To have more room for the dogs. The day I was to pick up the van, I arranged to go out to lunch with a friend who owns kennels as a Labrador Breeder to celebrate getting my new van. I noticed potholes on the way to her home, so, taking my friend back to her house after lunch, I decided to go home using the back road. Going along the road, near the river, I rounded a corner when suddenly I hit a washboard on the road. I tried to apply a little pressure to my brakes, but they did not work; my brakes failed me. "Dear Father, what is happening?" I cried out to Him as the van rolled over and down into the ditch, then rolled back again, stopping just short of the river. My plumber had seen what had happened and called the ambulance and fire department. When they came, they had to use the jaws of life to get to me. I had sustained another head and back injury. My doctor sent me straight down to the Halifax Infirmary.

Months later, I was able to get by with the help of a walker that my neighbor brought to me. Unfortunately, this was going to be another lengthy process of healing.

Joshua 1:9 Have not I commanded thee? Be strong, and of good courage, be not afraid, neither be thou dismayed. For the Lord, thy God is with thee, whithersoever thou goest.

CHAPTER 14

HEAVEN SENT ESTATE FOR DOGS

I started a kennel called the Heaven-Sent Estate For Dogs a year later. My neighbors helped me put up wild animal fencing around the whole area at the back of the house. Then a door was put into the back of the house so that the dogs would have easy access to come and go freely. My vet knew that I rescued Siberian Huskies and would call me if he had a husky brought into him in need of a home. I would travel down to pick the husky up and get them to their new home. This time it was a beautiful male Siberian Husky; it was love at first sight for both of us, so I called him Sheiko; we would have a special bond. The husky owner had brought him to the vet as he was covered in Porcupine quills and wanted the dog to be put down; however, the vet decided to operate on him to remove the quills. Then he phoned me to see if I could come down first thing in the morning to get the dog. In time I ended up with seven of these beautiful creatures. These beautiful creatures were so gentle and such lovely companions. Mickey, my shepherd, had died by this time, but I missed him, he had been such a beautiful, faithful dog, and I knew that Sandy missed him as they were always together. Every day we would go and walk the trails together, I felt truly blessed by the Lord.

Sometime later, I had arranged with my pastor to start a care group, as I had before, where we would meet, sing worship songs, study the Bible, and discuss whatever topic we were studying. We again met every Monday; it was an immense success, with people from the neighborhood and the village; usually around twenty people there. It was a lovely time together. After the meeting, we would socialize together and have refreshments.

During this time, I had a small job working for the Humane Society, selling dog licenses. I would use this time to meet with people and tell them what the Lord had done in my life. I met many people during this time. It was quite lovely; I met some beautiful people and was able to testify of the Lord in my life. On one of my calls to a man with a dog, who invited me in for a cup of tea, and as we talked, I could tell he was lonely, and his name was Doug; I asked Doug if he would be interested in coming along to one of Our care group meetings, he said yes, he would like to. I told him that they were held every Monday at 7 pm. Through these meetings, I found out that he was out of work. So, I asked him if he would like to do odd jobs for me? He very much appreciated it. One day when he came round to do work for me, he asked me if I would cut his hair for him? He had long blond hair, so I said I would. However, I would put a chair outside by the back porch, as I would not have him in the house with his shirt off.

Therefore, I started to cut his hair for him while quietly praying that the Lord would guide my words while Doug was under the scissors. I prayed, Lord, help me tell of the gospel of our Lord Jesus. Whenever Doug started to question or argue about what I was saying, I would say that he had better be careful, or his ear might get snipped by mistake. Doug started attending the Presbyterian church where I went. I invited him to get involved with the Bible studies at the church, which he did, and was extremely interested in them. I noticed that Doug was quite intelligent and gave good responses to the questions when asked about what we were reading. Doug and I became good friends, and he would help me out on the property and help me walk the dogs, which he enjoyed. We had a good relationship, enjoyable conversation and just enjoyed each other's company, which was something new in my life that I had not experienced before.

Doug's sister and family were lovely people, and I enjoyed their company, especially his nephews. Doug's sister Diane came to visit me. I had liked Diane and her family since meeting them. While she was with me, she said, "It is obvious that you and Doug are in love; instead of living separately, why don't you get married?" But get married? I do not know that I ever want to go down that road again. The next time Doug's family came to see me, the question came up again about us getting married. I knew Doug and I loved each other; I had never known that kind of love before. Doug was very romantic towards me; This had never happened before. Something new and wonderful was happening; where he would put music on, take me in his arms, and dance with me. Doug was extremely light on his feet and to dance with him was exhilarating. I decided to go with Doug and speak to the pastor and see what he had to say about this. Several months later, we were married under the apple tree in the front garden, with our friends and neighbors around us. It was simple but lovely. The church had let us borrow chairs for the people to sit on, and Doug's nephew had arranged fairy lights in and around the apple tree.

Did I take this to the Lord and ask of Him? I am not sure that I did. All I thought about during this time was that I was loved for myself, by someone with whom I could share the love of the Lord and have a conversation without being put down, plus we were so comfortable in each other's company. A relationship like this was something I had always wanted; it was so wonderful. We had been married for over a year; unfortunately, Doug was in and out of work. I could not understand this, as Doug seemed such a good worker. During this time, I was in the bathroom, off the kitchen when I heard shouting. I went to investigate. Doug was at the sink washing up and yelling that he heard me talking about him in the bathroom. I said, "But there is no one in the house except for you and me and the dogs." Again, he shouted at me and started coming toward me with malice on his face. I screamed and ran into the living room when suddenly I suffered a severe panic attack and collapsed. I came to and saw Doug's dad sitting in the armchair looking at me. Doug was back to his usual loving self. Confused, I looked at his dad, "What happened?" His dad said, "Didn't Doug tell you?" "Tell me what?" I asked. His dad said, "Doug has Schizophrenia. Is he off of his medication?" "What medication?" I asked; well, this was a shock, I had no idea, yes, he had funny moods now and again, but I left him to it, Schizophrenia? O no. Well, this explained the problem of not keeping his job. However, I loved Doug and was determined to try and help him with the help of our doctor. The medication messed him up, I knew Doug loved me, and I felt terrible for him. I wanted to help him in any way that I could.

Romans 8: 15 and 28 For ye have not received the spirit of bondage again to fear, but ye have received the Spirit of Adoption, whereby we cry Abba Father. 28. And we know that all things work together for good to them that love God, to them who are called according to His purpose.

We had been married for almost four years, and during this time, my Golden Retriever, Sandy, had to be put to sleep; cancer had gotten the better of her. I mourned that dog, so did Doug. Sandy and I had been through so much together. When she was gone, it was like a part of me went missing too. I now had Sheiko, Anika, Blue, and Buddy.

I had been to see the bank manager about re-mortgaging the house, and they had agreed to this to help me pay the bills, as Doug was rarely working, and my disability income was not enough. This Sunday, we had been to church and were invited back to friends for lunch. We had just finished lunch when I started not feeling well, and I knew something was not right with me. I said to Doug, "I think you had better take me home; I'm not feeling very well." So, making our excuses, we left. Getting into the car, I said to Doug, "You had better take me to the hospital; instead, something is very wrong with me." Our doctor arrived at the hospital, and as he examined me, touching my upper stomach, I screamed out in agony. The doctor went straight to the phone and called the surgeon on call in Amherst Hospital, then arranged speedy transport by ambulance to get me to the hospital. The pain was getting worse. Upon arrival in Amherst, the surgeon examined me and took an x-ray, showing that my Gall Bladder had burst, and crystals were going through my system. Immediately I was rushed to the operating theatre. After a long operation, the surgeon came to see me and said, "You were a fortunate young lady; you almost died; however, you are not out of danger yet, as your body is septic."

Nevertheless, I knew my God was in charge, and I was at peace knowing this. During my stay in the hospital, Doug came in with papers for me to sign from the bank; I was not very coherent in that my awareness of what I was signing was not clear to me; however, Doug insisted that I sign them, saying, "The bank needed them." Therefore, it shocked me when the bank contacted me to say that Doug was drawing a lot of money out of the account. I said, "How can that be? We do not have a joint account?" "You do," said the manager, "That paper was among the papers you signed."

CHAPTER 15

DISASTER

At Christmas, I arrived home from the hospital, still not well and in recovery mode. I was lying on the couch when Doug said, "I'll put more logs in the woodstove." I said, "No, Doug, it is fine," but he would not listen to me. Next, a mighty roar as the chimney caught fire. "O dear Father, not anymore, please?" Firefighters came rushing in and said, "The roof is on fire; you have to get out." Doug picked me up and half carried and dragged me to our next-door neighbors, about fifty yards away. It took the firefighters a long time to contain the fire. The force had melted the woodstove, and the room was an absolute mess. Thank you, Lord, that the dogs were outside and safe. Thankfully, I had insurance, which covered a new roof, a new woodstove, carpeting, cleaning, and painting. It was never as lovely as it had been. During this time, I was in a lot of pain from the operation, which left an enormous scar, and I still had not fully recovered from the Sepsis. After this, I was physically and mentally drained. "O Father, I need your help and guidance, plus your healing hand on me; I need You, please, help me?"

James 1:5 If any of you lack wisdom, let him ask of God, that giveth to all men liberally, and upbraideth not, and it shall be given him.

Later that year, Doug's income was not coming in as he was out of work again, so I had no help with the bills. I would buy groceries for a month; however, Doug would eat them up in a week. One evening, as we were sitting in the living room together, I was going over the bills in the ledger that I kept; I said to Doug, "We cannot go on like this, "Please stop taking the food, please leave it for mealtimes, as we cannot afford to keep buying groceries, as it has to last us. I am having a tough time making ends meet to pay the bills." Looking at Doug, I could see his countenance change, so putting away the ledger, I said, "I am going to get ready for bed." It was getting to be late in the evening.

I was in the bathroom to get ready for bed and had to go to the toilet; as I sat there, a sudden smash at the bathroom door and it burst open; in came Doug looking twice his size and blown up like a maniac. He started yelling at me, saying I was talking about him again, hitting me around the face and head. Next, Doug picked me up and dragged me into the kitchen, and threw me against the wall, beating on me the whole time. He opened the kitchen door and threw me down the stairs, banging against the stair rails as I was thrown to the back door, continually hitting, and yelling at me. He flung open the back door and threw me into the driveway; next, he flung the car keys at me and told me to get out and never come back. Buddy, the puppy, came out to me as I scrambled to escape. I had been screaming for help, but nobody came.

Getting into the car with Buddy, I drove to the neighbors next door, but nobody answered. Terrified, I cried out to the Lord, "Father, help me, what will I do?" Suddenly, the still, small voice of the Holy Spirit said, "Go to the police station in the village, there you will find a phone outside on the wall, pick it up and cry for help."

106

I was in hysterics by this time, and I had never driven so fast, terrified of what Doug might do. At the police station, taking Buddy with me to call for help, I picked up the phone; there was a police officer at the other end; I told her what had happened. She said, "Go back in your car and lock the doors and that a police cruiser would be there shortly." It seemed like an eternity; I was hurting so badly and could not stop shaking. Lights shone on my car as the police cruiser came alongside my car. The officers took me to the hospital, where I was treated and stayed with me. The doctor said to me, "I'm sorry, but we have no beds left for you to be able to stay here." I said, "I have a puppy in the car that will need me; what will I do? I will have to sleep in the car with the dog." The police officer said, "Don't worry, we are going over to your house to arrest Doug and take him down to the Bible Hill station; Doug will not be bothering you." A while later, an officer came to the hospital to tell me that Doug had been arrested and taken off to the prison in Bible Hill and that I would be safe at home. Tomorrow, the officers will come by to see me and let me know what will occur. So, after a while, still terrified, I was able to drive home with Buddy. Arriving home, my other dogs greeted me. It was soothing to be among the dogs; their love for me was paramount. I took care of them, and they took care of me. I praised the Lord for giving me these beautiful companions. I loved these precious dogs so much. They were soothing to my soul, hugging them to me. The next day, the officers came round and talked with me; they were so kind and thoughtful. They asked me if I wanted to go down to the Transition House for women? I said no, as I wanted to be with my dogs. However, I thanked them for offering this to me.

During the following weeks, going through notes in the house, I realized that Mike and Doug knew each other.

How can this be possible? I was shocked. How on earth could this happen? I thought to myself. Then realizing Mike's cunning ways, I knew this was possible. While over visiting my friend Donna, she informed me that she had a phone call from Mike, saying that he would blow up my house. I said to Donna, "Did you inform the police?" I asked her; no, she had not; however, while I was there, she did phone them and related the phone call she had received from Mike. Then more death threats followed. The police were immensely helpful and had known of Mike and Doug's alliance, so they agreed to keep an eye on my home and property. How frightening was this fact? Little did I comprehend that I would be under police protection until I left Canada.

Deuteronomy 31:6 Be strong and of a good courage, fear not, nor be afraid of them: for the Lord thy God, He it is that doth go with thee, He will not fail thee, nor forsake thee.

Letters from the bank started arriving, asking me to pay back my mortgage. I had been trying to pay down all the bills, but my disability payments were not enough to cover all the bills that came in. (Dear readers, you might wonder why I keep all my dogs? The answer to that is simple, they are my family, and I would instead go without myself where food was concerned than be without my dogs. At least I had freshwater, which I loved to drink, and fruit from the garden.) I found an auctioneer and asked him to come out and value all my furnishings and valuables that I had. When the auctioneer came out, he went through all the house, as I had some lovely colonial furniture. He said he would give me $7,000.00 for everything and arranged to come out with his truck to pick everything up. I would have no beds or bedroom furniture, no table or chairs or living room, dining room, or kitchen furniture, except my old couch and armchair, which the auctioneer said were not worth anything. However, this helped me pay off some of my debts for now. I would put a comforter and pillows on the floor and lay down with my dogs to sleep for the night-time. I slept well with them, and they would all curl into me.

Finally, I sought money counselling and met with an exceedingly kind man who advised me that I would not be able to pay the bills as I had insufficient income to do so. The counsellor put me in touch with a private trustee who would care for me for the next seven years. "O Father, not again, not another bankruptcy; what was I going to do, and where could I possibly go?" My lawyer was taking me Pro Bono, had, in the meantime, written to the government to get my name changed. The name change arrived a month later.

Colossians 1:23 If ye continue in the faith, grounded, and settled and be not moved away from the hope of the gospel, which ye have heard.

I started three days of praying and reading the Word of God and making notes of what the Lord was putting on my mind. Where was I going to go? I asked myself, and I started driving around looking for places for the dogs and me to live, without any success. Nevertheless, unbeknown to me, the Lord was working on my behalf. The following Sunday, while praying and crying out to the Lord, "Where shall I go?" That still small voice of the Holy Spirit said to me, "Phone Mary and Bill." These were my friends in Pugwash, Nova Scotia. "The still small voice of the Holy Spirit continued, they want to sell their house; ask them if they would be willing to rent to own their house to you?" So, I phoned Mary and Bill and said to Mary, who answered the phone, "Mary, I have been praying, and the Lord has asked me to ask you, would you and Bill be willing to rent-to-own your house. Mary said, "Let me ask Bill; I will phone you back." Less than 5 minutes later, the phone rang. Mary said, "How does $400.00 a month sound to you?" Then Mary said, "Bill has wanted to move to Amherst for some time; however, we haven't been able to sell the house. "Praise the Lord, Hallelujah, to my God." Bill and Mary moved me in that Friday; they had already rented an apartment in Amherst and had moved in. Through the trustee's help, I built up my credit again and eventually purchased the house in Pugwash some years later.

Psalm 91:2 I will say of the Lord, He is my refuge and my fortress: my God in Him will I trust.

CHAPTER 16

A NEW JOURNEY

In 2005, I moved into the cottage in Pugwash. I was full of gratitude for what the Lord had done for me. His faithfulness in hearing and answering my prayers the way He had. The Lord had far exceeded my hopes and prayers.

Proverbs 3:5-6 Trust in the Lord with all thine heart; and lean not unto thine own understanding, in all your ways acknowledge Him, and He shall direct your paths.

"Dear Jesus, I prayed, thank you for giving me this cottage and the land to go with it. I will love this home and bless it to you, and for You to reign supreme here."

I could not stop praising my Lord and Saviour, Jesus Christ. My heart was so full of love for Him. I was thrilled by His faith in me, a sinner.

I had bought with me some of the wild animal fencings and posts. The fencing I put up first to take care of the dogs and keep them safe. They had a good play area, which pleased me very much. I was still sleeping on the floor with my dogs as I did not have a bed or furniture except for my old armchair. I suddenly remembered the old funeral plan I had when I first arrived in Nova Scotia. Therefore, I phoned the funeral home to see if I was able to cancel my funeral plan and receive my money back? Yes, they can refund the money back to me. "Thank you, Lord," this would help me get some furnishings for the cottage. My friends found a bed put out for collection and brought it to me; after cleaning it up, the bed came up perfect. I just needed a mattress to go on it; this I found in a sale. Finally, I had a bed to sleep in again.

On my street was a Baptist church that I started to attend and eventually joined the choir. I made some good friends during this time. The pastor had teamed me up with a lady in the choir, Sheila was her name, and she was lovely, and we became firm friends. Sheila was an artist, and her paintings were marvellous. Over time, she would tell me her story. Sheila and her family had escaped from Burma and had made their way to Canada. I enjoyed being with Sheila; she was a warm, compassionate woman. We did a lot together going into Amherst and about.

The evening of the ministry went well. The choir was practicing new songs, as we would be going to New Brunswick to sing and minister to the prisoners there. We were able to do outreach with some of the prisoners. It was extraordinary in the prison and the routine we had to go through; however, this had to be.

I noticed Sheila was not doing so well, she did not want to eat her meals, and unfortunately, her daughter-in-law was putting unreasonable demands upon her, asking her to do this or that; it was too much for Sheila, and one day she collapsed. Sheila's daughter-in-law called the ambulance. Sheila was taken to the hospital; unfortunately, Sheila became weaker, refusing to eat, and finally, she died. On the day of the funeral, we were all mourning the loss of Sheila, as we all loved her. I missed my dear friend; I had known her for over two years. As time went on, something was missing in the church; I was so hungry for the Word of God. While at the hospital in Pugwash for an x-ray, I met a particular x-ray technician whose name was Laurie, who was always preaching the gospel; it did not matter who was there; Laurie would quote scriptures from the gospel. I knew Laurie was a Seventh Day Adventist and found out his last name and decided to phone him and his wife at their home. When speaking to Bev, Laurie's wife, I asked if I could go to their church. They said, yes, they would pick me up on Saturday to take me to church. I started on a wonderful journey with my Lord through this church, plus Laurie and Bev became fast, firm friends with whom I would go to church every Saturday. I loved the teaching and the love that was in the church. 2009 I was baptized into the church and have never looked back. Jesus became my husband, who loves me unconditionally and is my forever friend.

These beautiful people at this church helped me and did so much for me when I first started going to the church. They knew from Laurie that I had left some things at my previous home. I phoned the company in charge of my old house, as it had not been released for sale yet, and asked if I could go and collect some items that I had left behind? They said I could, so I let Laurie know, who arranged to go over to my home with some men. I would drive my car there. They brought everything back for me, including my old couch and stove. I started to renovate the cottage myself; however, I had a tough time with it as I only had a few tools. Laurie came by one day with another member and saw what I was trying to do. "You cannot do that," said Laurie, "Leave it, and I will come with some of the men, and we will take care of this for you." Which they did, they drywalled the bedroom, and where I was trying to seal up a door, one of the men built me a bookcase to go in the opening where the door was. They made a closet that I had tried to build myself with no success. They did a fantastic job for me, at no charge!

Later, with the aid of John, another member of the church, Laurie purchased and put in a stainless-steel flue piping and connected it to my stove so that I could have a fire and be warm. Again, they would not accept any payment for what they had bought and built for me.

When the men were coming in to do the work, I started to feel overwhelmed and had a tough time dealing with it all. This kind of goodwill was never given or shown towards me by man. It affected me, which deeply moved me that humankind could ever be this way towards me. Kindness was foreign to me; even now, I can feel and experience what I went through by typing this out. Feeling such worthlessness and wretched as a dirty rag doll. I had not met this kind of kindness before. I also had another dear friend from the church, Miriam, whom I had sat with at church; she was so kind and loving and, because of my interest in Ellen G. White, had given me books of hers, as she had duplicate copies that members of her family had bought. I felt so blessed by this and have come to love her writings. I had many dear and wonderful friends at this church; they were a real blessing.

One day walking around the vast lawn, I prayed Lord, show me how you would like the gardens to be. I next brought a pad and a pencil out to start sketching a plan for gardens and what to put in them. I wanted a lot of flowers; nevertheless, there had to be soft and hard fruit grown. I met a neighbor who raked the seaweed up from the estuary and asked him if he could deliver a load in his truck for me? He said yes, for $20.00, so I arranged for him to provide me with a load. I would have to let it sit for a year to get the salt out of it, and then it would be acceptable to use. I had planted my flower

gardens, and then I started to dig out a large trench 2'
deep and 8' square; this was for some of the seaweed
to go, then I would plant strawberries in it. I placed
the seaweed around the blackberries and raspberries.
I then dug seaweed into a hole where I wanted to grow
grapes. The fruit was produced in abundance. I would
be feeding my neighbors, and I filled my freezer with
fruit bags for the winter. I put in dwarf apple trees the
following year and planted salad foods. I Praise the Lord
for His abundance and grace that He showers on me.

Psalm 25:5 Lead me in thy truth and teach me: for
thou art the God of my salvation; on thee do I wait all
the day.

When first coming to Pugwash, I had gone to see the
Postmistress at the Post Office to let her know about
my circumstances in case Mike should turn up and
want some information about me. He had been there;
however, they are not allowed to give out information on
anyone, which made me so relieved. Mike had found out
somehow that I was in Pugwash but did not know where.
The Pugwash police knew about my circumstances and
were aware of Mike. Then letters started being left at
the Post Office for me by Mike; these I took to the police,
who said I would need another Peace Bond and would
have to go to Amherst to apply for one. I did not want
to see him again; I could not deal with that.

The dogs that I brought with me to Pugwash. My
beautiful Anika, a pure white Siberian, and Sheiko, a
beautiful grey, and white Siberian; Blue, a shiny dark
black mix with piercing blue eyes; he was a loveable
rascal; and my Buddy, who was a mixed Siberian/Lab.
These dogs were so precious to me. We had so much fun
together, taking them down to the beach for long walks
and playing in the water; I loved my dogs. One day, I had
gone out onto the deck at the back of the house, where

115

Anika was, she had bitten into her shoulder where a lump had suddenly appeared, and she was bleeding quite badly. I rushed over to my neighbor and asked, "Would you drive me to the vet as something is wrong with Anika?" My neighbor agreed; I sat at the back of the truck with Anika, holding a large towel around her. Arriving at the vet's, they took her in right away. I sat there crying, wondering what had happened. I did not have much faith in these new vets. The vet came out and told me; a blood vessel had been severed they could not save Anika; I was mortified; Anika was dead; she was only eight years old, this precious little girl of mine. I could not be consoled. Back at home, I sat on the floor with Sheiko and Buddy, and Blue hugged them to me and cried. Huskies are extremely sensitive to their owner's feelings, and I am sure that they sensed Anika was not coming home.

Working in the garden during the summer, I went to the shed for a tool; then, coming out of the shed, my laces caught on a tine by the door, I fell flat on my face on the concrete path. I screamed out for help, and then unconsciousness took over. The next thing I knew, I was moved onto a stretcher with a brace for my neck and my back. Then rushed off to the hospital with another head and back injury. According to my neighbors, afterward, the police came flying down thinking that Mike had attacked me. It was the police who ordered the ambulance men to put me into a brace. My face ended up all colors of the rainbow, and it was a wonder that I had not broken any bones. With the help of the Lord, after a while, healing was accomplished. He renewed me, and my strength came back.

Isaiah 41:13 For I the Lord thy God will hold thy right hand, saying unto thee, Fear not; I will help thee.

When I was healing, my Sheiko took to having seizures; I lay with him, comforting him and praying over him. Please, Lord, I prayed, take care of this precious dog of mine; nevertheless, Father, You alone know what is wrong with Sheiko; I pray, please, take care of him. He went back to sleep; however, the following day, I noticed that he had fallen over in the garden. I ran over to him and found that he was having more seizures. I phoned the vets I now had, told them of the seizures Sheiko was having and said I was bringing him down to them. With the help of a neighbor, I put a blanket under Sheiko to lift him into my car. We were only half an hour away from home when he started to have another seizure. I stopped the car and went to him; however, he died in my arms. O my Sheiko, I cried; you were my precious boy, how I had loved you. I turned the car around, drove home, and buried him alongside Anika in the garden. A year later, I was to lose Blue and Buddy. How hard was this to overcome? How I mourned for my precious dogs. I refused to be without a husky in my life; these dogs have meant so very much to me. Therefore, I went and rescued a beautiful black and white Siberian, and yes, I had to name her Anika. This little girl would be with me for a long time, and bless her, she followed me everywhere.

CHAPTER 17

A NEW LIFE

The year was 2013, and my uncle, who was in England, phoned and asked me if I would like to come for a visit to England and to bring my mother, who lived in Winnipeg. My uncle asked me to arrange everything, and he would send me the money, which he did. I contacted my mother and told her what her brother had said to me about going to visit him. Mum was extremely excited about it and said she would arrange with a friend to drive her to the Winnipeg International Airport. I would arrange a flight for myself to Winnipeg, where we would meet to fly to England. Everything was organized, the flights booked. I had asked my friend to look after Anika while I was gone for the two weeks. I drove my car down to Halifax airport to catch my flight to Winnipeg. I was to meet mum with her friend at a motel so that mum and I could ride the airport bus to take us to our departure. Everything worked out well, and we caught our flight to England. After almost eight hours of flying, we arrived at Heathrow Airport in England. I have always found Heathrow Airport a nightmare. Mum and I got left behind after leaving the plane. The trolley had forgotten to come for us. Our pilot was there, and he radioed for someone to get there immediately. My uncle and his son were waiting for us when we finally came through. When told of what had happened to us, he was not pleased and said he would complain to the one in charge.

During our visit with my uncle, he asked my mother if she was happy where she was living? Or would she prefer to move to another place? Mom said that a friend of hers had moved into this retirement home for seniors and said how lovely it was. Mum gave me the place's name, and I brought it up on my uncles' computer. It certainly was beautiful inside to look at, and as my uncle read through what they had to offer, he said to mum, "Would you like to move in there?" Well, of course, she would; there was no question about it. I then contacted the retirement home, spoke to the manager there, and asked if there were any vacancies? Yes, there were, so I arranged with the manager to email the forms necessary to get mum moved in as soon as possible. We had a wonderful time with my uncle and cousins, his two sons, and then visited my brother who lived in Wales. The Welsh countryside is beautiful, so very scenic with fantastic views in whichever way you turn.

Back at home in Nova Scotia, I took care of arrangements with my bank to set up a particular account so that my uncle could wire the money over to take care of the rent for mum. Benji, mum's dog, had passed away a while ago. Now, mum was with other people her age and she enjoyed it there at the retirement home. Mum loved it there and became very contented.

The following year 2014, again, my uncle phoned to ask if I wanted to go for another visit in the summer and bring mum along? He asked me to arrange everything again, only to use the money in the account that I had set up for him to pay for the travel arrangements. It was wonderful to see my uncle and cousins again. One day my uncle took mum and me down to his hotel in the New Forest. It was lovely and peaceful. While we were waiting in the lounge, my uncle asked me, "Would you like to come back to the UK to live?" I said, "That is my prayer and dream to come back." I had wanted to leave Canada for some time. As much as I loved where I lived, Mike had put a damper on it for me. To leave Canada and all that had happened would be fantastic. Five minutes later, he looked at me again and said, "Would you like to come back?" I said, "Yes, but I couldn't possibly afford to live here or buy a home in the UK." "Don't you worry," he said to me, "I will buy you a house; where would you like to live?" I gasped; my uncle would buy me a house, O Father, how wonderful, I thought to myself; I was stunned at leaving all the misery that I had experienced in Canada behind.

The next day, my uncle took mum and me down to Pembrokeshire, where my brother lives. I said to Laurie, "I'm coming back here to live." He gave me a big hug, and I said to my uncle and brother, "First we must find my church, then my home. So, Laurie went on the internet and brought up the Seventh Day Adventist Church in Carmarthen. I was so excited, and my uncle said he would take me down to see it. I was so grateful to the Lord for what He was doing for me. I realized that the Lord was using my uncle as a tool to get things completed in the way he wanted. The church was incredibly old and very Welsh; the whole setting around the church was so scenic, with a rushing brook to one side and lovely old trees around. By the time we arrived back at my brother's, Laurie had found a bungalow in an ancient Welsh village high up on a hill in Carmarthenshire. It was beautiful, and my uncle said, "I like the look of it; this is what you need; I will put in an offer." My eyes almost popped out of my head when I saw it; it was so beautiful with lots of gardens, which I love, and it is out in the countryside, which I needed. My uncle is a very generous man and always had been, and of whom I shall always be grateful.

My Father in heaven, You are so faithful to me; thank you for the mercy that you show towards me. Great is your faithfulness, O God unto me.

I arrived back in Pugwash, Nova Scotia, towards the end of July 2014. The houses in Pugwash were not selling, and those that did sell were selling at a loss. Nevertheless, I knew that God was in control of this whole situation, so I put my trust in Him completely. The first Realtor I quickly fired, realizing that he was not working in my best interest. Next, I asked a friend if he would look after the sale of the house. Peter had many people come through the home. During this time, I felt that the house would be sold and that I would be back in England again this year. I started to pack and box items that I would need to send over to England with that in mind. Then one day, this lady had an appointment to come through the house, and she spent a lot of time in the gardens that I had created with the help and guidance of the Lord; everything was organic. Strawberries, raspberries, blackberries I had in plenty. Gardens of beautiful roses and flowering shrubs. It had been a work of love. This lady wandered around, then came in and sank into my armchair; she had such a look of peace about her. On talking to her, she said that she worked out in the oil fields in Alberta and was looking for a home to retire in. I liked her and felt so strongly that she would be the buyer of my house.

The following day, my friend, the Realtor, phoned me to say that he had an offer on the house, he did not sound very upbeat, so I was surprised and delighted when he said that the offer on my home was $10,000.00 more than I had asked. He said that the lady was taking all my furnishings and that the closing date was for October 23rd, 2014. Now I was left with less than a month to get everything ready. However, I was not worried as I knew the Lord had everything in His control. The lady Realtor came to see me and could not believe all I was letting the lady have. Next, she asked me, "What are you doing about Anika, your husky?" With tears in my eyes, I said, I do not know; I explained how I had phoned the airport cargo to ask for the price of taking my dog, they said it would cost me $2,000.00, and I do not have that kind of money, as my uncle was taking care of the cost for the airline. He was not going to pay another $2,000.00 for Anika. Later that day, I received a phone call from the lady's Realtor to tell me that $2,000.00 was being posted into your bank account for you to take Anika with you. I could not believe the generosity of the lady.

Overjoyed, I praised the Lord, thanking Him for what He was doing. I got down on the floor and hugged Anika, saying, you are coming with me; tears of joy were in my eyes. I thought about what I needed to do. I phoned the vets and told them about the situation. They would prepare the papers for Anika to see the government vet in Moncton, New Brunswick. Then I had to apply for a pet passport for Anika. What a very crazy and exciting time. The airline had been booked, including my transfer plane, in Toronto. The $2,000.00 was in my bank, so I contacted cargo at the airport to book Anika in, giving them my flight number and times. They told me the size of the crate I was to buy for Anika and what to put in it.

On the 23rd of October, I had an appointment with my lawyer for the closing day of the house. I also travelled to Moncton with Anika to see the government vet. The government vet cleared Anika, and her passport was stamped so she would not have to go into quarantine. Then off to the pet store for her crate.

The 26th of October were the day Anika, and I was to fly out. My dear friends Laurie, Bev, and Gilbert were going to be driving Anika and me to Halifax International Airport. First, take Anika to the cargo area, where she will go into her crate and have all her papers checked. Well, we had a problem, the crate I was told to buy was too small, they would not allow Anika to go on the plane in the one I had bought. What was I to do? I was told you still have time to go to the mall and buy a larger one. Gilbert stayed with Bev, and Laurie drove me to the pet shop, where I purchased a giant crate. Then back to cargo to assemble it. Once this was done, Anika was on her way.

Arriving at departures with my friends, I found out my luggage was too heavy; next, I must either leave one piece of luggage behind or go to the shop at the airport to purchase a new piece of luggage. I did this; what a fiasco I had in the middle of the floor, transferring clothing out of one case into the new case. Underwear and all sorts were falling on the ground, in my panic to get things sorted out. Finally, everything was completed, and I said my goodbyes to my dear friends and was ready to board the plane. However, this is not all that happened. The devil was having a fun day with me, and he would not make things easy for me. The devil was not happy with the way things were turning out for me. There was going to be a surprise waiting for me at Heathrow Airport. Upon arrival at customs, even though I had my UK passport and papers, they said they had no record of me, and I had to go and sit in the guarded area until the customs cleared me. O dear Father, now what? I know that you are in charge.

Deuteronomy 31:6 Be strong and of good courage, fear not, nor be afraid of them: for the Lord thy God,

He it is that doth go with thee; He will not fail thee, nor forsake thee.

One hour later, the officer came up to me and apologized, saying that they could not find me in the records; however, after speaking to the head office, they relinquished me, and I was free to go. Thank You, Father. Looking around, everyone had gone; I thought, where is my luggage? It was up against a post, then I spotted a porter and asked if he could take me to the entrance, which he did. There were my poor uncle and cousin waiting for me. Oh, what a joyous reunion. Now to go and collect Anika. It took only ten minutes before she came out, then we were on our way home. Praise the Lord, Hallelujah!!

During the following months that I spent with my uncle in his beautiful home. Anika played with Digby, my uncles' Labrador, on his lovely estate. There were 3 acres of gorgeous grounds that his bungalow stood on. I was happy there with my uncle, spending time with him. Unfortunately, his younger son was causing a lot of problems for him. On one of these occasions, he attacked my uncle, thank goodness I was there to go in-between them and be able to phone the ambulance and the police. My uncle was severely shaken up. The paramedics took care of him, and after a while, he calmed down. His son had taken off to the train station to go back to his home. The police finally tracked him down back at his home and the police issued a warning to him. Having watched my cousin when I was there, he was showing the same signs and symptoms that my husband Doug had shown with Schizophrenia. I never knew if my cousin had been treated for this or not; nevertheless, my cousin proved to be very vindictive over the years to come to every family member. Unfortunately, my cousin was a loose cannon.

HOME

Early morning on the 19th of January 2015, accompanied by my uncle and cousin, we left Surrey in England to travel to Wales. Tears came to my eyes as we left England and travelled through the countryside of Wales; it was so beautiful; the hills and valleys were magnificent. After five hours of driving, we drove up to the old Roman village high above sea level, where my new home was. Upon seeing my home, tears welled up in my eyes; I could not believe that this beautiful bungalow would be my home. The home was so lovely, inside, and out. When I went out into the back garden to look at the view, it was far more beautiful than imagined. I looked out onto hills, valleys with sheep grazing, then looking out to the other side, there was the sea. Oh, Lord, I thought to myself, how beautiful is your creation. Thank You for bringing me here; you knew exactly what I needed—the peace of the countryside and beautiful gardens for me to work. Anika, my Siberian Husky, loved the garden and would go out and explore her estate, sniffing around all the hedges and shrubs that surrounded the outskirts of the gardens. She loved to lie in the sunroom and look out into the garden I could tell Anika was very contented, bless her heart.

In February, I decided to get a companion for Anika; I would have liked another Husky; however, the only ones they had at the shelter were two large huskies, and they would have to go together. The huskies were larger than what I was used to, and I realized they would be too much for me to handle. However, a young short-haired Retriever, whose name was Bailey, had been rejected by people three times in his short life. I, therefore, rescued him and brought him home to live with Anika and me. Bailey proved to be an excellent companion for Anika; he loved her and fussed over her. All this poor dog needed was to be loved and how faithful a companion he was to prove for me. The joy it gave me to see them run and play was terrific. I was so happy here and started meeting people and making friends, this was a loving community, and I have lovely neighbors willing to help out.

I had been attending my new church for some time and was asked by the Elder if I had taken the Sabbath School lessons in Canada? Answering the negative, I explained that women were not allowed to teach these classes there. The Elder was baffled; he could not understand why not? Then he asked me if I would like to start taking the Sabbath School lessons? I answered, yes, I would. Because of this, I was able to take on more responsibilities. Then one day, the Head Elder asked me if I would like to take a Lay Preaching course in Cardiff? My answer was yes; I would love to, as I felt the Lord moving in my life and realized that this was what He was leading me to. The course was fantastic, and I enjoyed it so much that I did not want it to stop. Unfortunately, the course had to end, and I received my Lay Preaching credentials. How wonderful this was.

The still small voice of the Holy Spirit came to me quite distinctively. When the pastor asked me to start preaching, I prayed, Father, You lead me in this. "What do you want my first sermon to be about?" "You must give your testimony first." "O Father," I prayed, "I cannot talk in church about my upbringing or first marriage; it was too awful." Again, the still small voice of the Holy Spirit spoke unto me, "Then, you must write a book on your life and how I have helped you."

It was two years ago, and constant prodding by the Lord has taken me since then to write this book. In October 2019, I first started my book, and now, the Lord has given me even more, to write about my life with this new edition. My holy family, Abba Father, Son, and Holy Spirit, have guided me every step of the way. My Father has known the agonizing periods of writing this book; however, without His help and guidance, I would not have been able to write this book. I give all Praise, Honour, and Glory to my precious holy family.

The year was 2019; Anika, my little girl, was ill and had to have regular treatments from the vets. I prayed, "Jesus, I do not want to be without a Siberian Husky in my life; these dogs are so precious to me. "Do you think I should get another Siberian already while Anika is alive? I looked on the Husky rescue site and applied for a husky; they were not forthcoming, so I went back and prayed again. "Jesus show me what to do about a husky, please?" The Lord put upon my heart (Many Tears Rescue). I looked on their site, and right there was Blusie, a large black and white Siberian; I thought, dear Lord, you knew. I applied for Blusie, and she was home with us within two weeks. What a beautiful, gentle creature she is, and what she had suffered through, being used for breeding, and having her puppies taken from her. Blusie would need a lot of care and nourishment to get her back into shape. While Anika was alive, Blusie would lie down beside her; I know she sensed how ill she was. It was Anika's time to take her to the vet; she was too precious to me, and I could not let her suffer. Anika had been such a faithful companion, and she will be sadly missed. When I look at Blusie, I see Anika; they are so much alike; Anika used to lie down beside me when I was preparing food or whatever; now Blusie does the same thing, except Blusie is a larger Siberian. Now the Lord has given me another faithful companion in Blusie and Bailey.

It is the year 2022, and I have grown more in the Lord by searching His Word in the Bible and the sermons that He has given me. These sermons have enabled me to know more of the Lord by searching the scriptures and what He has been teaching me. It has helped me understand the incredible journey with Jesus from Genesis and the creation through to the Revelation of Jesus, the last book in the Bible. The world's history and how the Lord worked in the lives of Enoch and Noah, who walked with God, the Patriarchs, and the Prophets, all the way through the Old Testament and New Testament. How Jesus paid the ultimate price for us on the cross at Calvary, and that all who believed in Him would be saved.

John 3: 16-17 For God so loved the world, that He gave His only begotten Son, that whosoever believeth in Him should not perish, but have everlasting life. 17. For God sent not His Son into the world to condemn the world, but that the world through Him might be saved.

EPILOGUE

Due to a Serious Accident in 2020 and a Stroke in 2021, I can no longer drive a car. However, I still go and preach in my church, through the blessings of dear friends who will drive me to church each Sabbath. Nevertheless, the Lord continues to lead me on a wonderful journey with Him.

Look for my next book to be published, the DIY Lady and how the Lord helped me through my accident in 2020 and again my stroke in 2021. He is still leading and guiding me on a journey with Him

Our dear Lord and Saviour know of all the hurting, aching hearts out there. What my Lord and Saviour have done for me, He can do for you too, if only you will Trust Him and Believe in Him. If you do, like me, you will never look back. Go forward with our dear Lord and Saviour, He is holding out His hand for you to grab hold of. Do not let go, keep holding on to Him, for He loves you.

With the help of Jesus, you can learn to forgive those who have hurt and abused you in your life. When I was able to do this, I was set free, no more bitterness, no more grief. Let our precious Saviour help you and you too will be set free.

If Jesus can forgive us for our terrible sins, how much more should we forgive others.

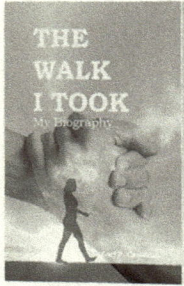

THE WALK I TOOK:
MY BIOGRAPHY

By Lori P. Cameron

The Walk I Took: My Biography is an in-the-furrow memoir written by Lori P. Cameron, and one which sails through the author's life as she confronts a troubled childhood which was marred with emotional abuse from her alcoholic mother, along with turbulent adult relationships from abusive ex-husbands – and how she eventually paws out with God's help as she learned how to live a fulfilled life of love and forgiveness.

With a judicious and astute cover page and a striking prologue, Lori dedicates the first chapter of the book to her poignant childhood as she bares her soul and pulls you into the hostile environment she grew up in, her pain, her frustration, and utter desperation. Her early years of adulthood saw her fall into the hands of two cruel and coercive men who had glaring weaknesses prompting her to take a redemptive walk from these heart-wrenching relationships through an inspirational journey of redemption and building a solid relationship with Jesus.

The author bravely peels back the mask highlighting complex but sensitive issues seldom discussed using her life as a kaleidoscope. Throughout, the book shines with the love of a caring Father whose love overflows. Readers will experience all kinds of emotions reading this unvarnished biography that ripples with intensity as the author writes with intimacy and unflinching honesty and encompasses these with a conversational tone. This creates an indelible package for readers to screen through and sop up the numerous takeaways present in this tapestry.

The book's infusion of Biblical Scriptures and melding these with the litany of events that the writer chooses to discuss, accentuate the story within creating essential elucidation for all who read this text. Few books and individuals have the power to change a life. This book, and what God is doing through it, is one of those rare cases. It serves to remind us that we are not alone in our struggles and that Jesus is with us through these storms.

The Walk I Took: My Biography is unequivocally an indelible cathartic biography fused with life coaching from a quintessential voice with a story to tell.

Reviewed by: Lily Amanda

Milton Keynes UK
Ingram Content Group UK Ltd.
UKHW041023090823
426580UK00001B/92